NO ONE COMES CLOSE

J A Newman

AUTHOR'S NOTE

Out of respect for the people concerned I have used fictional names to protect their identity.

NO ONE COMES CLOSE

Part One

NEW YEAR'S EVE 1986

I'm sitting on the bed in the dark, trying to block out the noise from downstairs – Mal and his parents laughing and joking together, drinks being topped up ready for midnight, while the *Hogmanay Show* blares out from the television. Somewhere in amongst all this is fifteen year-old Grace, probably not far from her granddad.

But I can't go down there and play happy families – Mal and I have drifted apart over the years to the point where he spends most of his leisure time at the pub while I work evenings and weekends, mobile hairdressing, hoping to amass enough money to be able to leave him.

Not for the first time, my thoughts run back down the corridors of time to Ron – his blue-grey eyes always slightly amused; his appetite for life. In a dizzy moment I had sent him a fortieth birthday card; the 9th December etched onto my memory along with his parents' address. I had no idea where this would lead but I willed the card to reach him, wherever he was.

Every morning I have rushed to pick up the post but every morning I have been disappointed. It's nearly twenty years since I last saw him. Maybe he's not even in this country?

Mal shouts up the stairs. 'You coming down? It's nearly midnight.'

'In a minute,' I shout back.

But I stay rooted to the bed and dab my eyes, delve into my memories and unwrap the evening I first met Ron.

I was seventeen.

MONDAY 12 SEPTEMBER 1966.

Marie and I joined the queue, paid our entrance fee and had our hands stamped with the invisible marker. In the cloakroom, surrounded by a fog of hairspray, three girls elbowed each other for a piece of the mirror while applying layers of mascara and giggling over who they might meet tonight.

We handed our coats to the assistant and quickly gave each other the once-over.

'You look nice, turquoise suits you. New shoes?' asked Marie.

I looked down at my square-toed black patent. 'Yeah, I shouldn't really but they were in the sale; only thirty-nine and eleven. I like your dress. Is that the one you got in The Clothes Peg?'

Marie nodded. 'Red again, I know, but I love it!'

We jostled our way through to the bar, bought our drinks and managed to find two seats at a table in the corner of the hall. We chatted about things that had happened in the salon that day until the lights dimmed and Chris Barber and his Jazzmen took to the stage.

After enjoying the first few numbers, Marie's infectious laughter signalled Geoff's arrival. They had only been dating for a few months but were already talking of getting engaged. At seventeen – and Marie was even younger – this was the furthest thing from my mind. And I couldn't understand what she saw in him; he seemed rather ordinary compared to her.

We clapped and tapped in time to the different rhythms while a few couples jived. Thirty minutes into the performance the band announced they would be taking a break after the next number. *The Sheik of Araby* gave way to *Reach Out* by The Four Tops. Geoff offered to look after our handbags while Marie and I made our way onto the small crowded dance floor.

'I thought you said Geoff was at night school?' I shouted, trying to make myself heard above the loud speakers.

Marie beamed and shouted back, 'It was cancelled.'

We got into the groovy beat, Marie provocatively swaying her hips for Geoff. In the semi-darkness I scanned the hall and wondered if I would meet anyone tonight. Some of the local boys looked my way but I looked away. I had never wanted to go out with anyone local.

The Beatles *Gotta Get You into My Life* suddenly resonated around the hall. After a few moments I was aware of someone beside me, jigging to the beat.

'Hello,' he shouted, 'on your own?'

'No. I'm with Marie.' I pointed in her direction. She flashed us a smile.

He shook his head. 'That's not what I meant. What's your name?'

'Julie.'

'Mine's Ron. You'll probably think this very corny, but do you come here often?'

'Yeah, most Mondays.'

He nodded, took a sip of his beer. Even in the dim light I couldn't fail to notice his alert pale eyes, fair hair and tall slim outline.

The music stopped. I looked around for Marie; she was sitting at the table with Geoff. I went over to pick up my drink. Ron followed, pointed to my glass. 'What're you drinking?'

'Oh, only port and lemon.'

'Looks like cherryade! Want another?'

'Please.'

We pushed our way to the counter and waited. The bar-staff were flat out.

He pointed again to my drink. 'Want something stronger?

I shook my head. 'This is fine, thanks.' I didn't want to give the wrong impression.

I'd had an embarrassing experience last New Year's Eve: Pam, one of the girls at work, had invited me to a party. Being very naive, I thought a party meant food, so I purposely went without dinner. I was the only single girl there and they kept taunting me – 'Sweet sixteen and never been kissed,' and shouting, 'Don't let the side down, Julie!' while I sank another whisky on my empty stomach. They all thought it hilarious when I vomited all over the sitting room carpet before I could find the bathroom.

Pam's husband ran me home at two in the morning. Before I knew what was happening he was all over me. I felt powerless but finally managed to get out of the car and stagger up the path to our front door. He was suddenly there beside me asking for another kiss. Somewhere deep inside I knew it was wrong, but I was too drunk to hold him off. However, I was conscience-stricken the next day when I was too ill to go to work (no public holiday for New Year in those days) and beside myself for having earned my father's disgust.

I cast the thought aside and watched Ron as he caught the barman's attention. Ron. His name didn't suit him; it belonged to someone older, more ordinary, like one of our neighbours. But somehow I knew, for me, the name Ron would always be synonymous with this animated person.

I heard Marie's voice behind me. 'Aren't you going to introduce me?'

Ron turned, took a mouthful of beer and carefully passed my drink over to me.

'Thanks,' I said, 'this is Marie.'

She flashed him her brown-eyed smile and I felt an unusual twinge of jealousy. They shook hands. Geoff was hovering behind us; I introduced him then he sank back in the shadows.

'I don't suppose you've seen my mate Lofty, anywhere?' asked Ron. 'I don't know how I've lost him; he towers above everyone!'

'He's probably in the next bar,' suggested Marie.

Ron took another gulp of beer and led me through to the brightly lit saloon bar where we found Lofty on the far side.

'Pleased to meet you, Julie,' said Lofty, in his brown velvet voice. He must have been all of six foot six.

Ron saw my reaction and said, 'I'm waiting for, "*what's the weather like up there?*" That's what people usually say.'

Aware of my silly grin, I looked down at my feet.

'Do you live around here?' asked Lofty.

I nodded. 'Not far, just up the road.'

'Not like us,' said Ron, 'I expect you've picked up the Hampshire accent? Full of oohs and ahs.'

'Oh, I wouldn't say that.' I felt my cheeks burn under his gaze and took a sip of my drink. 'So, what brings you here?'

They exchanged glances. 'Work mainly,' said Lofty, 'but we heard the music was good at the Black Prince so we thought we'd give it a try.'

'Yeah,' said Ron, 'beats hanging around the digs!'

'Oh? Where's that?'

'Catford Bridge. It's nothing much but it's somewhere to lay our heads at night.'

Chris Barber's jazz band was again in full swing and people were beginning to drift back into the hall. Lofty bought another round of drinks and the three of us made our way to a vacated table. As I listened, I couldn't imagine living and working away from home. Ron did most of the talking while Lofty kept an eye out for any attractive girls. It became obvious Ron loved his hometown of Petersfield but there was little or no work to speak of. The bright lights of London had attracted them but I got the impression it wasn't matching up to their expectations. They had landed themselves in dead-end jobs – Ron was working at a textile firm and Lofty at a furnishing store – and both were desperately trying to keep up with the rent.

All too soon the evening was drawing to a close; from the hall came the sad hollow sound of the band packing away their instruments. People were drifting out to cars, waiting for buses.

Ron checked his watch and downed the rest of his beer. 'We ought to be making tracks, too, Loft.'

'What time is it?'

'Just gone eleven,' Ron stood up and turned to me. 'Can I walk you home?'

'Yeah, I'll just get my coat. Meet you outside?'

He nodded. 'See you at the station, Loft.'

I queued impatiently for my coat hoping Ron would still be there when I came out. I couldn't exactly say what it was, but he was different to anyone else I had been out with. At last the attendant handed me my dog-tooth coat, I threw it on and ran outside. Ron had waited; he was smoking a cigarette and watching the last of the cars leaving the car park. As we crossed the road and walked briskly up the side streets, I watched the yellow streetlights casting our two moving shadows on the pavement; his a little taller than mine. We walked in virtual silence until I asked him if he would be able to get a train at this time of night.

Full of confidence, he said, 'Oh, yeah. Last one's at midnight.'

I slowed my pace and stopped at our wrought iron gate. He glanced at the Victorian facade of our five-bedroom house, then at me. 'You live here?'

I nodded.

He gently tilted my face up to his. The kiss caught me by surprise and sent a delicious kick through my body. His eyes lingered on mine. 'See you at the same place next Monday? Will you be there?'

I nodded again.

'Which way's the station from here?'

'Turn left at the end of the road and keep going till you get to the baker's. The station's on the opposite side. You can't miss it.'

'D'you wanna bet?' His mischievous gaze swept my face as if trying to commit my every feature to memory. He kissed me again, softly, and a knot of excitement hit my belly.

'Well, must dash or I'll miss my train. See you next Monday. Don't forget!'

I watched him hurry to the end of the road, willing him to turn round. Then, just before he disappeared from view, he turned and waved. I waved back.

Aware of the late hour, I let myself in as quietly as possible, hung my coat on the hallstand and went through to the breakfast room. Mum was still up, sitting at the dining table reading the *Evening News*.

She looked up. 'Hello, Ju. Did you have a nice time?'

'Yes, I met someone. His name's Ron, comes from Petersfield.'

'Oh? Where's that?'

'Hampshire.'

'Huh, he's a long way from home.'

'He's got digs at Catford. I gave him directions to the station.'

'Oh?' she was only half listening, engrossed in the newspaper. 'Will he get a train at this time of night?'

'Mm, last one's at midnight.'

Mum turned to look at the wooden clock on the mantle piece. 'He's cutting it fine.'

I smiled; I knew Ron would catch his train. 'Well, I'm off to bed; another busy day tomorrow.' I kissed her on the cheek.

'Yes, sleep well, love. I'm turning in soon. Oh, will you have time to do my hair on Friday?'

'I should think so. I'll check in the book tomorrow. Night, night.'

I ran up to my bedroom; one of Bach's Brandenburg Concertos was faintly audible from Dad's studio. I knew better than to intrude – he would be bent over his drawing board, carefully filling in meticulously drawn letters with Indian ink, for a piece of advertising; just the angle-poise lamp and his music for company.

I closed my door, sat in the pale green tub chair in front of the dressing table mirror and watched the smile spread across my face.

Ron.

*

Since that night I had continued to meet Ron at The Black Prince on Monday evenings but he let me down a couple of times. One evening I waited outside for half an hour in the freezing cold. I finally gave up and went home when neither he nor Marie showed up. Ron's reason this time was that he'd been moving to a flat in Vauxhall and couldn't let me know.

Ron had started coming to the house on Wednesday evenings and brought his records to play on Dad's hi-fi – a privilege that implied I was capable of being trusted with this precious piece of equipment. I had grown up with the sound of Dad playing his jazz or classical records in our big front room on Sunday mornings and sometimes he would play the Boogie-Woogie on our upright piano. On the odd evening when he didn't have any homework, I would quietly sneak in and sit with him in the subdued light to soak up the atmosphere, while he sat engrossed in Beethoven or Mozart with a glass of 'gin and it' in his hand.

One evening Ron brought Ravel's *Bolero* with him and we sat on the settee in front of the electric fire, moving in time to the infectious beat.

'What d'you think?' he asked.

'Yeah, I like it.'

'I first heard it at school. It had the same effect on the whole class. They couldn't help tapping and clapping anything in sight! Even the desk lids were banging up and down.'

'Really?'

He nodded. His gaze fell on my lips and I felt the spear of excitement as he tilted my chin. We had the room to ourselves all evening but he never tried anything; his hands never wandered. I was unsure whether I wanted them to or not.

Ron's other choices included the sound tracks to *The Big Country* and *The Magnificent Seven*. I was happy to listen, eager to know more about him and what excited him. One of my favourite pieces was the romantic theme from the soundtrack of *Genghis Khan*. In the last scene, after the final battle with his arch enemy Jamuga, Genghis Khan is slumped on his throne against the vast Mongolian landscape, bloodied and exhausted. He tells his wife, Bortai, *'I want that God should see me in the face.'* She orders two of his men to turn his throne into the wind. The music plays out as she holds his hand and he quietly slips away. No matter how many times I heard it, the very poignant and beautiful music engulfed me with emotion and I wondered if it had the same effect on Ron. I did hope so.

OCTOBER 31 1966

Halloween at our house had become a momentous occasion. Every year the neighbours' children went home dripping wet after bobbing apples. However, in recent years, they'd got the game down to a fine art and came armed with their swimsuits. Dad decorated the breakfast room with bats cut out of thick black card hung from the ceiling, and flames cut from black and orange crepe paper stuck to the picture rails. My sister, Louise, and I had the job of hollowing out the swedes, faces cutting into them and placing candles inside. These sat outside on the gateposts. When the party was in full swing, Dad would put an old white sheet over a mop and emerge from the cellar making ghostly noises, sending the children into a frenzy.

By six o'clock the excitement was mounting.

I went to the kitchen to see if Mum needed any help preparing the buckets of water for the bobbing apples.

'I'm fine, Ju. Just keep Herbie off the cakes, would you?'

My little brother shot me a cheeky look and put his hands behind his back. I wagged a finger at him and wandered along to the hall, eager for Ron's knock on the door. I checked my vampire make-up once more in the mirror – white greasepaint on my face, thick black lines round my eyes, blood red lipstick and wondered what Ron would say.

On the hall table the telephone rang. I picked up the receiver.

'Julie?'

My heart sank. 'Yes.'

'It's me, Ron. I er...I'm afraid I can't make it tonight.'

'Oh.' My excitement ebbed away to a pool at my feet. There was a long pause as he tried to think of something else to say. I swallowed and caught sight of my vampire face in the mirror. It suddenly looked absurd. I sat heavily on the bottom stair.

'Yeah,' he began, 'I'm really sorry, but the truth is I'm skint.'

'Oh.'

Another awkward pause.

'I can't make it on Wednesday, either. I know I said I'd come down but... I just don't have the money.'

The burden of double disappointment made me crumple into a heap.

'But er...I'll see you next Monday, OK?'

I managed a response and ran upstairs to wipe off my make-up, tears mingling with the cleansing cream. I was so looking forward to the evening with Ron and seeing the surprise on his face as I opened the door. Now he wasn't coming.

I could hear the front door banging and excited children trooping through the house, the opposite of my mood. I sat for a few minutes reluctant to join in, then realising everyone would be asking after me, I reapplied a little make-up and went downstairs.

Dad frowned. 'All right, love?'

I nodded and swallowed my sadness.

'You sure?'

I took a deep breath and let it out slowly. 'Not really. Ron just rang – he can't make it tonight.'

Dad went to put his arm round me but not wanting the others to see I was upset, I drew away. 'I'll be OK.'

He smiled and gave me a wink.

I followed the excited voices to the kitchen where Mum was judging the fancy dress. I left them to it and retreated to my room. I could hear a lot of giggling then the inevitable screaming when Dad came out of the cellar with the white sheet. I smiled to myself; how easy it was to be a child.

Twenty minutes later the telephone rang again. I ran downstairs and picked it up.

'I just had to ring you back; you sounded so upset. Listen, I've got around the problem for Wednesday. How about meeting me on Charing Cross station at seven-thirty? We could see a film or something?'

'All right. Whereabouts on Charing Cross?'

'Under the clock, you can't miss it!'

'Ok. See you Wednesday, then.'

I was already planning what to wear. Time would soon go – when I woke up in the morning I would only have to wait another day before I saw Ron again.

The children were still shrieking with laughter. The kitchen floor was awash.

Dad looked across at me. 'Did he ring back?'

I nodded. 'I'm meeting him on Wednesday at Charing Cross.'

He smiled. 'Mm, I see.'

I beamed at him.

WEDNESDAY 2 NOVEMBER 1966

It was my day off so the hours dragged, my thoughts on little else but meeting Ron on Charing Cross. By 5 o'clock I had so many butterflies in my stomach there was little room for the eggs and bacon Mum had cooked for me.

Feeling confident in my outfit – a blue dress, my favourite dogtooth coat, black patent shoes and handbag – I boarded the train and chose a forward-facing window seat. At New Eltham more passengers crowded on. Not wanting to catch the attention of a businessman who sat opposite me, I stared through the window into the dark night. My reflection stared back at me. From the edge of my vision I watched the man take out a biro from his breast pocket. He kept looking at me then I realised he was drawing my portrait on his newspaper. Sitting still as a statue I covertly watched him in the reflection of the window, trying not to smile. I felt very flattered but my shyness would not allow me to ask if I could see the finished sketch. He suddenly replaced his biro and sat back with a smug expression all the way to London Bridge.

My skin prickled as the train pulled into Charing Cross. I opened the door to the echoing sound of whistles blowing and carriage doors slamming. Walking quickly towards the ticket barrier I scanned the crowds for Ron. I spotted him under the huge clock – the designated meeting place – wearing a beige knee-length raincoat, navy trousers and black lace-up shoes. He was smoking a cigarette and observing people as they rushed past. Recognition lit up his face when he saw me walking towards him. I felt lighter than air.

'You didn't get lost, then?'

'Nope.'

He trod on his cigarette, took my elbow and guided me towards the underground station. 'Would you like to see *The Ten Commandments*?'

'I'd love to.'

16

I was astounded at how well he knew the underground: up and down escalators, on and off tubes, through draughty subways. I was being carried along on a tidal wave until finally we came out into the cold night air and the bright lights of Leicester Square. To me, the West End was a glamorous place, especially the Odeon cinema with its dazzling frontage.

I felt very privileged as we took our seats eight rows back in the stalls and settled down to watch Charlton Heston, Yul Brynner and thousands of extras in this epic film that had been made in the previous decade. I had already seen it at the Regal in Bexleyheath but nothing compared to the sense of occasion in this cinema and sitting next to Ron made it doubly special.

'Are you enjoying it?' he asked, handing me a tub of ice cream during the interval.

'It's wonderful.'

'Good. I thought you'd like it.'

We talked about other classic films we'd seen and it was obvious we shared the same tastes.

After sitting cocooned all evening in the warm cinema, we came out to a cold wind, hurried along to the underground and boarded the tube back to Charing Cross. The station was a lonely place late at night and I was thankful when Ron waited with me on the platform. We huddled in a corner out of the wind.

'Have you enjoyed yourself tonight?' he asked again.

I nodded. 'I always do when I'm with you.'

He drew me close and I melted into his long, sensuous kisses. *I love you* flashed up on the inside of my closed lids. But I couldn't tell him. Not yet.

He saw me onto the train and slammed the door. I pushed down the window. He gently brushed a strand of my hair aside and gazed into my eyes. 'I'll phone you tomorrow.'

The train began to pull us apart. 'See you on Monday in any case,' he shouted.

I waved until his image disappeared and my train snaked into the night.

MONDAY 14 NOVEMBER 1966

Every evening I willed the telephone to ring, but every evening it remained silent. It had been almost two weeks since that night in town and I was becoming increasingly depressed at the thought of never seeing Ron again. Marie was worried about me. This afternoon, while we were clearing up the salon and hanging out the towels, she had asked me to meet her and Geoff at the Black Prince this evening. I told her I wouldn't be much company.

'You let me worry about that. You can't keep moping about at home, you know. He's got no right, treating you like this. I bet he goes out with other girls; that's why you haven't heard from him.'

This thought niggled like toothache. I hoped she was wrong.

At seven-fifteen Marie jumped off the bus and we hurried along to the Black Prince. I kept looking out for Ron although I knew it was unlikely he would show up. We handed our coats in at the cloakroom and quickly checked our reflections in the long mirror. Then, coming out of the cloakroom I turned round and almost bumped into him. I froze.

'Fancy seeing you here!' he said, as if I was a casual acquaintance.

I was speechless. Felt hot and cold all at once.

'I'll see you in there.' He had his hand stamped then went to the men's cloakroom.

Marie watched him go and looked at me. 'He's got a nerve turning up like that.'

I shook my head. 'It's OK.'

'Well, I think you're mad. Aren't you going to say something?'

Ron came up to us. 'Here, let me buy you both a drink.' He began to guide me towards the bar. I looked round at Marie and hoped she wasn't going to make trouble.

'Don't worry about me,' she said, 'you two go ahead; Geoff'll be here in a minute,' and sure enough in walked good-old-dependable Geoff. 'There. Told you! See you later.'

I sat at a table while Ron went to the bar. I watched him. I could almost see the excuses forming as to why he hadn't been in touch.

He brought our drinks over. 'Do you want to dance?'

'In a minute.' I wanted an explanation but was frightened to confront him in case he finished with me. I instinctively knew he didn't want a possessive girlfriend. My insides were in knots. My cheeks were burning. How could he act so...normal?

He avoided my gaze, took a gulp of his beer. 'I expect you wanna know where I've been, what I've been up to.'

I nodded.

'Yeah, thought you would.'

I looked at him. He looked away and took a long drag on his cigarette. Blew the smoke up to the ceiling, tapped the packet on the table. 'I tell you what – how would you like to come down to Petersfield for Christmas?'

I was knocked sideways.

'You don't have to tell me now. Think about it.'

I finally found my voice and mumbled something about always spending Christmas with the family.

'Yeah, of course... I can understand that.' He looked everywhere but at me. 'OK. Well, what about Boxing Day?'

I nodded. 'I'd like that.'

'Good. That's settled, then.'

We enjoyed the rest of the evening and I tried to forget about what he'd been doing and who he'd been with for the past ten days. He said he'd walk me home. I suggested a walk through the park – it was more secluded.

He grinned cheekily. 'Oh? What do you have in mind?'

My cheeks flushed, I wanted to come back with something witty but couldn't. We walked to a small sheltered spot. All was still, not the slightest breath of wind. Trees stood in the street light like an audience waiting for our passion play to begin. He swung me round to face him. I felt his lips on mine and a string plucked deep down within my belly.

He held me at arms' reach, eyes full of merriment. 'I feel like doing something mad!'

'Like what?'

'Oh, I don't know,' he cast around and spotted the church on the opposite side of the road, 'like climbing that church steeple!'

'And how would you do that?'

He shrugged. 'No idea!'

The church clock suddenly intervened, striking the half hour.

'Blimey, is that the time? I've gotta go or I'll be catching the milk train!

Please, not yet.

He gently tilted my chin. The anticipation alerted every nerve in my body.

'Listen,' he said, 'how about meeting me on Wednesday like you did before?'

'On Charing Cross?'

'Yeah. In the meantime, I'll think of somewhere for us to go.'

I nodded, already on Charing Cross in my mind's eye.

'OK. Right now I really DO have to go.'

'See you Wednesday.'

'Yeah. Don't get lost!'

WEDNESDAY 16 NOVEMBER 1966

'I thought we could go to the Motor Show,' said Ron guiding me along the subway. 'My favourite car at the moment is the MGB.' He showed me a picture of the bright red sports car on the front cover of his glossy *Motor* magazine. It looked very glamorous. I tried to memorize it.

We entered the oppressive atmosphere of the underground platform; crowds of people jostling for position. Then a draught and the tube screeched into the station. Everyone surged forward anxious to scramble on and we got parted. I grabbed the swinging handle and tried not to get my feet trampled on. Each time the train lurched I was thrown against a man in a gabardine raincoat or a woman with shopping bags. I looked across at Ron; he was grinning.

The tube finally stopped at Earl's Court and I pushed through the crowd eager to get to Ron before I lost him. We hurried along subways and up escalators.

Ron smiled, 'Not used to this, are you? Ha, you soon will be!'

The Earls Court exhibition centre was huge and brightly-lit, thronging with people all clambering to see the sparkling new models. The metallic sounds of car doors and bonnets being slammed down echoed all around; some of the cars stood on high platforms, others on the floor. Ron spotted the MG stand and dragged me over to it. We joined the queue for a chance to sit in the gleaming red MGB with its hood down.

Ron finally got a turn and I watched him going through the gears, oblivious to everything but the car. In his mind he was out on the open road. 'Yeah, this is the one for me,' he said at length. 'Pity I can't afford it! Wanna go?'

He moved across to the passenger seat while I tried to keep my mini skirt in place as I slid into the driver's seat. I gripped the leather steering wheel.

'Here,' said Ron, 'I'll show you how to work the gears. Put your foot on the clutch.'

I did as he asked while he pushed the gear lever into first, second and third.

'Go on. You try it.'

I did, but felt self-conscious under the glare of staring eyes. I tried to *feel* the gears and change them smoothly. Since August I had been learning to drive in an Austin 1100 but this gear lever was minute in comparison and felt very different.

'Where shall we go?' he asked, imagining the road opening out before us.

'I don't know but I think we ought to get out and let someone else have a go. Look at the queue.'

'Nah, don't worry about them!'

He eventually looked at the crowd and went round to the driver's side to open the door for me. I tried not to look ungainly as I climbed out. Ron's eyes glinted cheekily and his mouth twitched. I felt my cheeks flush.

He took my hand and led me over to the new Aston Martin DB6 with its bullet-smooth lines.

Ron shook his head. 'Nah! That's serious money. I'll leave that one to James Bond.'

'My brother's got a Dinky model of the DB5. The ejector seat really works, the doors open, and it even has the defence shield at the back and guns at the front,' I gushed, hoping to impress.

'Really? Huh, kids these days – don't know how lucky they are.' He quickly changed the subject. 'You hungry?'

I nodded, but I wasn't. I wanted him to take me away from the crowds; just him and me.

'I know a nice little place not far from here.'

We hurried down some side streets, lamp-light spilling onto the rain-polished pavements. We came to a bistro called La Barcia, stepped inside to sultry warmth and waited.

A plump woman dressed in black emerged from the kitchen. 'Table for two?'

'Yeah, thanks,' said Ron.

She showed us to an intimate brick-clad corner. I glanced around. On the tables stood lighted candles in dusty wine bottles, wax dripping down their necks. Fishing nets hung from the ceiling and draped the walls. I wondered how Ron could afford to bring me to such a place when most of the time he didn't have the price of his train fare. He handed me a menu. I stared at it.

He threw his down on the table and sat back. 'Well, I know what I'm having. What about you?'

I had read in a woman's magazine, that if you were taken to a restaurant and weren't sure what to order, to ask for the same as your date. But I instantly regretted it when he told me he was ordering chicken curry with apple pie and custard to follow.

'I love food,' said Ron. 'Some people eat to live – I live to eat! They do a great curry in here.'

Two huge platefuls of curried chicken quarters with rice were delivered to our table. In no time at all Ron had finished his but I was struggling with mine. I didn't want to leave any as he was paying and felt awkward as he watched my every mouthful.

'I soon won't be a teenager anymore,' he said, out of the blue. 'It's my birthday in a couple of weeks.'

'Oh? What date?'

'Ninth of December; it's a Friday.'

'Will you be doing anything?'

'Oh, yeah, I'll be at home – I'll make sure of that – out with my mates and Lofty.'

I hadn't expected him to be quite so blunt. I think he sensed he'd said the wrong thing.

'I've been on the phone to Mum and Dad; they're looking forward to meeting you on Boxing Day.'

'Oh, good. I'm looking forward to meeting them, too.'

'Yeah, you'll love Petersfield.'

The woman came to take our plates and soon returned with the dessert. I picked at mine but Ron scraped up the last of his apple pie and custard and looked covetously at mine. I pushed it towards him but he politely declined.

On the way back to Charing Cross, he briefly showed me another club he frequented with his mates from the flat, called Bungee's Coffee House; a dark smoke-filled, basement with sticky tables groaning under the weight of empty bottles and glasses. I could hear some great Blues being played somewhere in a back room and would've loved the chance to experience it, but Ron looked at me, then at his watch. 'Nah, come on, you'll miss your train.'

On the platform we stood away from the draught and the prying eyes. His kiss sent me into that dark sensuous dimension only he could take me to. I wanted to stay there forever but he suddenly snatched me back to reality. 'This is getting to be a habit!'

My train trundled in and stood waiting. Once again, time had slipped away like sand through my fingers.

*

JANUARY 5 1987

I pulled onto the drive and turned off the headlights. Exhausted after a busy day and evening, the kettle beckoned. My breath plumed in the frosty night air as I humped my hairdressing box up the path and let myself in. Canned laughter from the television drifted through the closed living-room door. I shut out the night, dumped my box and hung up my coat.

On the hall table the telephone rang. I picked it up.

'Julie?'

'Yes?'

'This is Ron, your old boyfriend from twenty years ago, phoning from Sydney, Australia!'

Shock and disbelief swept through me – this wasn't happening. I mumbled a response, my heart pounding against my ribs as I listened to his Australian accent mingling with undertones of original Hampshire.

He sounded full of excitement. 'Gee, it's really good to hear your voice. How are you?'

I could hardly breathe. 'I'm fine thanks. And you?'

'Yeah, I'm well. I got your card.'

'Oh, good. I wondered.'

'Yeah, what a surprise that was! I'm sorry I haven't rung before but it took its time getting here. It went to Mum and Dad's old address. She forwarded it on to me here in Sydney.'

'Really? That's amazing.'

'Yeah.

There was so much I wanted to ask him but I was anxious that Mal might come and ask me who was on the phone. I knew he was sitting only a few feet away the other side of the closed door, so I kept my voice down.

'So tell me – where are you living now?' Ron asked.

'A village called Melbourn, near Cambridge.'

'Fancy that – another Melbourne, eh? You married?'

'Mmm. And I've got a daughter.'

'That's great. How old is she?'

'Fifteen.'

'Does she look like you?'

I smiled. Grace was a carbon copy. 'Yeah, tall and slim with blonde hair.'

There was a pause while he pondered this.

'And what about you?' I ventured, trying not to let my voice reach fever-pitch.

He cleared his throat. 'Been living with a girl for ten years, but er... looks like that's coming to an end.'

A tiny flutter of hope danced at my shoulder.

'So, what's Melbourn like? Funny your village should have the same name as a town here in Australia!'

'Yeah, it's fairly small, in the middle of lots of flat open space... a bit like the Prairie.'

'Yeah? Sounds quite rural, like Petersfield. Not at all like our Melbourne.' There was that familiar chuckle.

'No. How are your Mum and Dad?'

'They're well. Oh, and guess what? I'll be seeing them later this year. I'm coming to England in April for a month; I'll look you up!'

The breath caught in my throat.

'You and your husband,' he added. I wondered if he meant it. The thought of him coming here and my having to explain...I couldn't picture him with Mal. It was all wrong.

'My sister Sally's birthday's coming up soon. And I know yours is at the end of the month. I'll send you a card.'

He'd remembered! But how would I explain that one?

'Lucky you caught me,' I said, 'I've just come in from doing a perm.'

'Ah, you're still hairdressing, then?'

'Yeah.'

'Busy?'

'Mm, out every day and most evenings....got my own business.'

'That's great.'

Suddenly stumped for words and anxious that Mal might burst out of the living room, I reluctantly cut our conversation. 'Yeah, anyway, it's really lovely to hear from you.'

'You too, Julie. I'll keep in touch. You'll be getting a card through the post. Look after yourself.'

The telephone call lasted all of three minutes but seemed more like twenty. I couldn't believe I might see Ron again; but on reflection, I shouldn't have put my phone number on the card – it was a silly thing to do.

My heart was leaping up in my throat. My legs felt weak but the thought of Mal in the next room wiped the smile off my face. I checked in the hall mirror for any change to my demeanour and tried to hide my excitement.

Breathe. Act normal.

I poked my head round the door. Mal was laughing at *Only Fools and Horses*, a big leg swinging over the arm of the chair. I was on the point of closing the door again, but he looked up at me.

'All right?'

'Yeah, busy. I'm going up for a bath. Where's Grace?'

'Round Claire's. They're walking her back later. Want your back scrubbed?'

'Ok. Give me twenty minutes?'

He nodded.

I closed the door and flew upstairs, hovering three feet above myself. Ron had phoned me! And after all these years he still wasn't married!

As I sank into the hot foamy bath, a big smile spread across my face.

BOXING DAY 1966

My alarm shrilled at six-thirty but I was already awake. This was the big day; I was going to Petersfield to stay with Ron and meet his Mum and Dad. Almost two whole days with Ron! I jumped out of bed, turned on the three-bar electric fire and started to get ready. I could hear movement downstairs and knew Dad had got up to see me off.

As I entered the cosy warmth of the breakfast room, Dad came in from the kitchen carrying a cup of tea. I marvelled at the way he always looked so well groomed, even in his dressing gown and pyjamas. Rimless glasses, dark hair swept back Clark Gable style, a neat moustache.

'Hello, love. All ready?'

'Mm, I think so. Just got time for some breakfast. Mum still in bed?'

He nodded. 'I'm taking her a cup of tea; I expect she'll be up soon.'

'She should be having a lie-in after yesterday.'

He smiled and went along to their bedroom which was on the ground floor, leaving me to contemplate the train journey and the next two days – the unknown. What were Ron's parents like? He hadn't told me much about them. I hoped they were friendly. I tried to imagine Petersfield, a sleepy little town nestling in the green hills of Hampshire.

Dad had made some porridge. I helped myself to a bowlful with sugar and milk and managed to force it down along with half a cup of tea.

Dad came back. 'You know, I think your mum's a bit worried about you making this journey.'

'Huh! Anyone would think I was emigrating! I'll be back tomorrow evening,' I said, trying to sound more confident than I felt.

'You are only seventeen, love.'

'I know. I'll be careful.'

I went up to clean my teeth then checked for the umpteenth time that I had everything in my case. When I came down, Mum was standing there wearing her long, red corduroy dressing gown. Her honey-coloured hair was in need of a comb-out and I regretted not having the time to do it for her.

'You all ready to go, then? Everything packed? Toothbrush?' asked Mum.

I nodded.

'I hope you have a nice time and remember, always get into a carriage with other people; you never know…'

'She'll be all right, Joyce. Have a good time, love. Any problems, just give us a ring, OK? Got enough money?'

'Yes. Thanks, Dad.'

I kissed them goodbye in the hall, picked up my case and handbag and felt their caring eyes following me down the path. I turned and waved and closed the gate behind me. They waved back and waited until I was out of sight before closing the door.

It was still dark as I made my way to the station, my heels echoing on the pavement, every step taking me closer to Ron. My only company was my moving shadow thrown by the yellow street lamps.

On the opposite side of the road, in the churchyard, the tall colourless trees swayed slightly in the breeze. With a stab of guilt I remembered I hadn't been to church for months, my excuse being that I was too tired to get up early on a Sunday morning after standing on my feet all week. Mum never pressed the point, unlike Marie's Irish parents. Marie regularly attended Mass on Sundays and even went to Confession in her lunch hour. Thankfully my parents were not so religious – my dad had his own views on religion. He said it was like one big club where the entire congregation was hoping to buy a front seat in heaven. 'You don't have to go to church to pray,' he'd say, 'you can pray anywhere, even in the toilet. God doesn't mind.'

I passed the row of semi-detached houses, street lights reflected in their dark windows, and hurried along, pinching up my collar against the cold wind. Making my way down the hill, the little parade of shops came into view.

A memory of meeting Dad from the station after work flashed into my mind: riding my maroon fairy bike down to the village and propping it against the baker's window, listening for the train doors slamming and the train slowly moaning up the track as it left for its next stop. Waiting for the tall upright image of my dad to emerge from the stream of people; his briefcase in one hand, whilst swinging his walking umbrella with the other. His fedora slightly tilted and his calf-length camel overcoat worn with style. His open smile when he noticed me would make my heart leap. Sometimes I would go down and meet him without my bike, hold his hand all the way home and watch his spit-and-polished shoes beating on the pavement.

When I was a child, train journeys to London meant Selfridges and Hamley's toy shop at Christmastime or days out to Trafalgar Square and visits to the News Theatre to watch the Warner Brothers cartoons, and feeling very grown-up sitting on a bar stool in Lyon's Corner House eating lunch.

The station held a new connotation for me now: this train would be whisking me to Waterloo, a change, then on to Petersfield to meet Ron and his parents.

Under the harsh dead light of the ticket office, I approached the window. 'A single to Waterloo, please,' my over-loud voice echoed. The man silently produced a ticket and went back to his newspaper.

My footsteps reverberated in the dank subway as I made my way to the opposite platform, hoping for the shelter of a warm waiting room. I was out of luck. The stale cigarette smoke hung on the cold morning air, the cast iron grate full of dog-ends. The cracked green tiles of the hearth exposed white veins. I shivered.

Thankfully it wasn't long before the train rumbled along to a standstill. I rushed out to meet it but the carriages were all empty. I chose one and got in.

Soothed by the motion of the carriage, I began to imagine what the next two days held in store. Ron had been vague about any plans. But I reminded myself how eager he'd been for me to see Petersfield and a smile tugged at my lips.

I counted the now familiar stations and as the day began to dawn, I watched the suburbs morph into the grey city buildings of London Bridge; a short wait and on to Waterloo. The enormous station was springing to life – whistles shrilling, carriage doors slamming, people rushing about. I found the ticket office and bought my ticket for Petersfield.

'What platform, please?' I asked.

'Four.'

'How long will I have to wait?'

'Next one's eight minutes past.'

I looked at my watch and hurried along. There was a train standing at platform four so I checked with the porter that it was the correct one. He nodded, blew his whistle and signalled to the driver. I walked briskly along peering into all the carriages but I still couldn't find one that was occupied. I chose one, put my case up in the luggage rack and settled into the fuzzy brown seat. The porter blew his whistle again. But just as the train was leaving, an elderly man, wearing a military style overcoat and flat cap, sat opposite me and dropped his knapsack by his feet. There was no corridor so I couldn't look for another compartment. Remembering Mum's warning I sat rigid and stared out the window.

The man frowned at me. I closed my eyes, but opened them again – that was the wrong thing to do – I wouldn't be able to see him coming at me. I sat transfixed and pretended he wasn't there and relived the few times I had gone back with Ron to his digs at Vauxhall in a shabby terraced house shared with three other lads. Worn-out, pre-war furniture in the kitchenette, cramped bedrooms and an outside lavatory at the end of the back yard. On the landing was an unused wash hand basin, and from it, green algae ran down the wall. Ron tried to laugh it off but I could tell he was ashamed of his lodgings.

One evening, while I sat in the threadbare armchair trying to ignore the stale coffee cups and fish and chip paper strewn on the table, Lofty came in and pointed to my tapestry skirt. 'My mum's got some curtains like that!'

Ron found this hilarious. My white lace tights were also called into question, but I enjoyed being the focus of attention and got the impression my fashionable image was much talked about.

Ron and I often went to the cinema to watch the latest films, but some evenings we were left on our own in the flat. Sometimes I would sit and listen to him playing his guitar. He favoured the American folk songs of the Deep South and I loved listening to *Freight Train* that he played so well.

Some evenings he would take me upstairs to lie with him on his single bed under the window, the glare from the street lamps intruding on our privacy. There was never any mention of sex, but to bask in his closeness was enough. However, one evening I felt brave enough to pull out his shirt so I could run my fingernails over his back.

'Oh,' he breathed, 'don't stop.'

'I've grown my nails especially for this purpose,' I whispered.

'It's a very good purpose.'

His moans of passion were beautiful but scary – I'd heard horror stories of girls getting pregnant without doing very much. But I needn't have worried – time was against us once again and when I gently told Ron it was time to leave, he hastily tucked his shirt back in as if the house was on fire. When I relived this moment alone in my bed, I wondered – given more time, would we, could we have gone any further?

My train lurched to a stop. The man sitting opposite suddenly stood up and peered through the windows at the signs for Godalming. He got out and banged the door and I heaved a sigh of relief and unlocked my arms and legs. At least I wouldn't have to worry about my return journey – Ron would be with me as far as Waterloo.

Finally, the train pulled into the sleepy little station of Petersfield. I handed my ticket in at the gate and walked through the ticket office, my heels clonking on the floorboards. I found Ron walking towards me; his warm smile made me quicken my pace.

'Hello, how are you?' he said.

'Fine, thanks.'

'I bet you were up at the crack of dawn? Here, let me take your case.'

'I was up at six-thirty!'

'Crikey! I was still in the land of nod, then! My brother-in-law's offered to give us a lift.'

I watched the way Ron's hand held my case and the way he walked and rejoiced that for the next twenty-four hours I would be in close proximity.

A tall dark-haired man got out of a Morris Minor and shook hands with me. 'Hello, Julie. I'm Martin, pleased to meet you. Did you have a good journey?'

'Yes, thanks.' I wanted to forget the strange man in the carriage.

Ron held open the back door for me and passed me my case. He then sat in the front passenger seat. I wondered why he hadn't sat with me, but I ignored it and watched the pretty countryside drift by until the car stopped on a small drive outside a neat semi-detached house. Ron opened the door and took my case.

'See you later,' he said to Martin.

Ron led the way through back door, into the kitchen and through to the welcoming front room where his parents sat either side of a roaring fire.

Ron stood my case on the floor. 'Mum, Dad, this is Julie,' he grinned. 'I know you've been dying to meet her!'

His mum, a little woman with short wavy hair and a neat appearance, rose to her feet. 'Hello, love. I'm Lottie.'

I held out my hand.

'Ooh, your hands are cold! I expect you'd like a nice cup of tea after that long journey? I've got the kettle on.'

'Yes, please. That would be lovely.'

'Let me take your coat.'

His dad was next. 'Sit down, Julie. Warm yourself by the fire. Make yourself at home – we don't charge!' He had a kind open face and horn-rimmed glasses. 'So, you're a hairdresser then, Julie? Can you do anything for me?' he joked, stroking his bald pate.

Lottie came in with cups of steaming tea on a tray and set it on the coffee table.

'Take no notice of Jack; likes to think he's funny.'

His dad grinned and winked at me and I realised this was their usual form of banter. I began to relax.

Lottie lifted her eyebrows at Ron and shot me a glance; it seemed she approved of the girl her son had invited. We made small talk and drank our tea until Ron handed me a floppy parcel in Christmas paper. 'Here. I've got you a present!'

'Oh, I've got one for you, too,' I said, and jumped up to fetch it from my case. I handed him the small wrapped box and sat with the present he'd given me.

His mouth twitched. 'Well, aren't you going to open it?'

All eyes were on me. A flimsy royal blue nightdress slipped out of the Christmas paper. It surprised me. His parents exchanged glances.

'Thank you. It's lovely.' I smiled, hoping the reason for my blush would be mistaken for the warmth of the room.

Ron opened his Cedarwood after-shave. 'That's great, thanks. I'll wear some of this later, but right now I want to take you out and show you some of the countryside. Coming?' He took my hand and I welcomed the chance to escape the awkward moment. He handed me my coat and shrugged into his jacket.

'We'll see you later,' he called over his shoulder.

'Yes, all right, love,' Lottie followed us out. 'Are you taking the truck?'

'Yeah.'

'Wait, let me put a blanket on that seat.' She turned to me, 'I'd hate you to spoil your nice clothes, love. Jack's been using that truck at the wood yard.'

How thoughtful.

The day was crisp and bright; a pale blue sky with a hint of purple on the horizon. I watched the low sun strobe through the trees at the side of the road and highlight the remains of the snow on the grass verges.

Ron pointed at the sky in the distance. 'Look, a flock of geese!'

The birds flew in formation, the sun tipping their wings. In the fields the dark winter trees were silhouetted against the bright blue sky and I could see why Ron loved 'God's country' as he called it. Looking back over the short time I had known him, it was hard to believe I was here with him now. Would this be a regular occurrence, going home with him at holiday times?

'Well? What d' you think?'

'It's beautiful. I can understand why you love it so much.'

'Yeah, wait till you see it in summer!'

Did that mean I would be coming back, then? He smiled at me and I felt an overwhelming love for him. I knew that all too soon, these two days would pass into my scrapbook of memories.

Ron explained that Mapledurham, which comprised Buriton, Petersfield and Sheet, was mentioned in the Doomsday Book. This historic town took its name from St Peters in the Fields, the church that stood at its centre.

'How wonderful,' I said. '*We* have a church mentioned in The Doomsday book, too, St Mary's.'

'Yeah? That's great.'

We stopped at the vast green heath and I imagined how beautiful it would look on a summer's day – people enjoying the boating lake, children on the swings...

'We'll have to get back soon,' Ron said, looking at his watch. 'Mum'll have the dinner on.'

The little house was a hive of activity when we got back – Ron's brother and sister and their spouses had arrived. Pots simmering on the stove, Lottie mopping the steamy windows. The delicious aroma of festive fare made my mouth water.

Ron introduced me to his sister who was carefully carving the remains of yesterday's turkey on the kitchen table.

'Sally, this is Julie.'

Her grey eyes twinkled. 'Hello, Julie. I've heard a lot about you! I expect he's been showing you the sights?'

I nodded.

'Where's Madge?' asked Ron.

'Not sure. Back porch, I think.'

He went through to find her. 'Here, Madge, leave that for a minute, there's someone I want you to meet.'

A little woman with short dark hair came through, wiping her hands on her apron.

'Hello, Julie. How are you?'

'I'm fine, thanks. Do you need any help?'

'No, that's all right; there's enough of us out here already. I'm sure you'd rather be with Ron!'

'Yes, go on, off you go,' agreed Sally, 'plenty of time for cooking and chores. Enjoy yourself while you can!'

Ron took me through to the front room and introduced me to his brother Robert who closely resembled his dad. Madge, Sally and Martin soon joined us. A room full of happy smiling faces – it seemed they were going out of their way to make me feel at home.

Lottie announced dinner was ready. We all went through to the little dining room and took our places; Ron looked up at me and smiled, as if to say, 'You'll enjoy this.'

I had always felt self-conscious eating in front of strangers but this gathering put me at ease. The cracker jokes caused much laughter around the table and I gradually felt as if I'd always known this family. The meal was delicious: cold roast turkey and pork, crispy roast potatoes and all the trimmings. I declined the Christmas pudding and cream but Ron devoured his and asked for more.

That evening, Ron took me to a party at The White House, a huge Georgian property in its own grounds on the edge of town. Loud rock music greeted us as we approached the steps to the stone-pillared porch. The double doors stood open onto a huge hall with high ceilings and a black and white tiled floor. Most of the rooms held clusters of people deep in conversation with drinks in their hands. But the one with its door closed was where the music was coming from.

'Lofty should be here somewhere,' said Ron, and pushed open the door. The room was dark and heavy with stale perfume. I caught a glimpse of some clothing on the floor. Ron pulled me away and closed the door. 'I don't think we'll be staying here too long.'

We left our coats on an overloaded rack in the hall and continued looking for Lofty. We peered into one dimly lit room where people sat all around the edge on big floor cushions, talking in hushed tones and smoking weird-looking cigarettes, but no Lofty. Then we came upon a room being used as a bar.

'Well, we might as well have a drink now we're here,' said Ron. He found some beer for himself and poured me a glass of wine from one of the many opened bottles on the table. He recognised a big man dressed in black accompanied by a thin little woman with mousy hair that hung down her back like a curtain. The man took a drag on his cigarette, blew the smoke up to the ceiling and looked me up and down. 'How long have you been going out with Ron, then?'

'Four months,' I blurted out, knowing full well I could tell him the exact amount of days and hours.

The man lifted his bushy eyebrows and nudged Ron. 'Four months, eh?'

'Huh, yeah,' Ron looked awkwardly at the door.

Unable to break the tension I stared into my drink. The big man dragged his silent little girlfriend across to the other side of the room where he found someone else to talk to.

'Come on,' said Ron, 'let's go. I can't see Lofty anywhere and he's not the sort of bloke you can miss.' He drained his beer and started to lead me outside. As we passed the dimly lit room he remarked, 'This isn't exactly my scene and I know it's not yours.'

We rummaged on the rack and found our coats. It had begun to rain. He quickly let me into the truck then opened the driver's door. He sat brushing the rain off his hair whilst fumbling with the controls on the ancient heater. 'Are you cold?'

'Yes, a bit,' I said, wrapping my coat around me.

He drove us out of the grounds. 'I'll stop in a minute. At least the wipers work!'

We stopped in a lay-by but he still couldn't get any heat into the cab. I snuggled further down into my coat.

'Bloody thing! Never mind; with a bit of luck we won't need it. I'll keep you warm.' He put his arm round me and gently turned my face to his. Our lips met and my heart turned over. 'I'll drive you up to the heath,' he said, 'looks beautiful at night.'

He was right. The moonlight shone into the cab and highlighted the rain-spattered windscreen like jewels. Somewhere far off an owl hooted and I felt the thrill of anticipation as Ron moved closer, his eyes heavy with desire. I melted into his kiss and felt the searing love-shard pierce my belly, every nerve in my body reaching out to his. At that moment I willed time to stand still – no one had ever made me feel like this. I had to tell him or I would burst.

'I...I think I love you.'

I waited for his response. There was nothing. I wanted to claw back the words, turn back the clock. He drew my head to his shoulder and stroked my hair. I knew I had broken the spell.

'Say something,' I heard myself whisper.

He let his hand drop from my hair. Unspoken words hung in the air.

Finally, he said, 'I'll tell you when I'm ready, but for now, let's just enjoy what we've got.'

My heart dropped heavily. I felt sick.

He looked at his watch. 'Better make a move, I suppose. It's getting late.'

Silence sat between us like an unwelcome passenger on the journey back to the house. He pulled onto the drive and banged the door of the truck leaving me to get out on my own. I followed him indoors.

We were alone in the kitchen, save for Marmaduke the big ginger cat. I bent down to stroke his thick fur and relished the soothing touch of the animal against my legs.

Ron went to the fridge, poured two glasses of milk and handed me one. 'I'm gonna put some cream in mine. Want some?'

I shook my head.

He drank his milk and fed the last of it to the cat while I stared at mine. It was turning sour in my stomach. I felt cold, although the room was warm.

Then, as if someone had flicked a switch, Ron said, 'I'll bring you up a cup of tea in the morning, then I can see what you look like in that nightdress.'

I felt the blood return to my cheeks. 'I could have died this morning!' I went to give him a playful slap; he caught my wrist and pulled me towards him. This time the kiss was passionate and rough. It surprised me.

'Better get off to bed,' he said at length, 'Don't wanna take things too far.'

I followed him upstairs and we said goodnight on the landing.

He lifted an eyebrow. 'Don't wake Lottie and Jack!'

I went to my room feeling confused.

I undressed. The cold nylon of the royal blue nightdress cascaded over my body and chilled me to the core. I swallowed down the turmoil of emotions – was it anger or dismay I was feeling?

I turned back the blankets to reveal a welcome hot water bottle. Hugging it to me, I silently thanked Lottie for her thoughtfulness and snuggled down in the bed. I tried to switch off my busy thoughts but the scene on the heath would not dissolve.

DECEMBER 27 1966.

I awoke early, listened for movement downstairs and waited in bed for Ron to bring me the promised cup of tea, but neither Ron nor the tea materialised.

Lottie was in the kitchen when I went downstairs, so I went to say good morning. There was no sign of Ron.

'Did you sleep all right, love?' asked Lottie, filling the kettle and setting it to boil.

I nodded. 'Thank you for the hot water bottle.'

She smiled. 'Well, I knew you'd want one. It was cold last night, wasn't it?'

Yes, more than you'll ever know.

We made small talk while she busied herself with the frying pan. The smell of eggs and bacon brought Ron out of hiding. He sauntered in as if last night hadn't happened and went to the sink to wash his hands.

'Truck needs a bit of work so I thought I'd see to it.'

I nodded, speechless.

The two of us sat awkwardly at the table, the only sound coming from the cutlery scraping our plates. Ron mopped up the last of his egg with a slice of bread, got up and went outside to mess about with the truck again. I cleared the table and helped Lottie wash up. I welcomed the activity – it calmed my thoughts.

Ron and I met Lofty in The Sun at lunchtime. This was a pleasant little country pub in Buriton. Ron seemed very popular with the locals and I got the impression the family were well thought of. Ron and Lofty ordered pints of bitter, I had a shandy. I sipped it slowly; it relaxed me and settled my stomach. But Ron joked with Lofty about certain things that had happened over Christmas, while I felt abandoned like last year's Christmas present.

We had dinner at Lottie and Jack's without the rest of the family. Ron's parents were so friendly and willing to please that I didn't want to offend them by leaving any of my meal, but I struggled with every mouthful. The atmosphere between Ron and I was very strained; I only hoped Lottie and Jack hadn't noticed. We went back to Lofty's to play cards in the afternoon but Ron ignored me as if I was invisible. I was feeling very uncomfortable with all this; I didn't know what to do or what he was thinking.

Ron dealt another hand and looked at his watch. 'We'll have to make this the last one. I don't want to miss that train.'

Shouldn't he have said *we* don't want to miss that train?

He got up to leave. 'See you later, Loft.'

Lofty nodded and smiled at me.

I followed Ron out to the truck and we drove back to the house in silence. I went upstairs to collect my things. Lottie and Jack were in the hall waiting to say goodbye when I came down.

'Well, it's been lovely to meet you, Julie,' began his dad, 'two days soon go, don't they?'

'Yes, they do.'

'Come and see us again, love,' said his mum.

That depends on Ron.

'I will. Thanks for everything.'

Lottie fussed over Ron, anxious that he'd picked up his clean washing. 'Sure you've got everything, love?'

'Yeah, thanks mum. See you at the weekend.' He threw his canvas knapsack over his shoulder with the names of his musical heroes biroed onto it: Pete Seager, Bob Dylan, Paul Simon. He kissed his mum on the cheek and she smiled at us. 'Have a good journey.' She patted Ron on the shoulder. 'See you soon, love.'

At Petersfield station I bought my ticket for Waterloo while Ron stood with Lofty. When the train arrived I was thankful Lofty got into a different compartment. Ron and I had one to ourselves but he sat opposite me and kept his distance. My coat slipped off my knee at one point, exposing more leg than usual. I covered it back up.

'Oh, I was just enjoying that!' he said, grinning.

I don't understand you.

On the platform at Waterloo, the cold struck deep into my soul but instead of drawing me close, Ron stood on his own and lit a cigarette. He was fidgety, looking everywhere but at me. When the train came thundering in he planted a glancing blow of a kiss on my cheek and muttered, 'I'll phone you, Thursday.'

I boarded the train and looked round for him. But he was gone.

FRIDAY 30 DECEMBER.1966

Marie and I went to lunch in Hide's department store. I was glad of her company; it took my mind off things until she began to question me.

'Come on, what's wrong?' asked Marie, glancing up from her sausage, egg and chips.

'I wish I knew.'

Her big brown eyes bore into me. I didn't have to tell her it was Ron.

'He said he was going to phone me last night...'

'Is he still messing you about? He doesn't deserve you. If I were you, I'd forget him and find somebody else...'

'...It's not that easy.'

'Isn't it?'

I shook my head and looked down at my plate. 'You don't know him like I do – I can't explain how I feel.'

'I've got a pretty good idea.'

I didn't think anyone had ever felt like me. Ron was different, special, and I didn't want anyone to tell me otherwise.

'It's all too one-sided if you ask me.'

'I'm not asking you.'

Marie put her knife and fork down at looked at me. 'I'm sorry. You know what I'm like – can't hold my tongue.'

I nodded. 'I'm sorry, too. I know you're only trying to help.'

'Come on, let's finish this and have a look round the shops.'

We bought a few lingerie items in the sales and went back to work, but all afternoon I couldn't help wondering why Ron had given me that seductive royal blue nightdress without making any more reference to it.

NEW YEARS' EVE 1966

I'd had a busy day in the salon with customers wanting flamboyant hairstyles for the New Year, but I was in no mood for celebrating. It looked as though 1967 would be pushing its way in without me hearing from Ron. Where would he be tonight? Who would he be with? Marie was seeing Geoff, of course, cosily watching the television together like an old married couple, talking of saving up. It all seemed rather dull to me. For all Ron's strange behaviour, I still wanted him.

At six-thirty I jumped off the bus and ran home, battling against the biting wind. I thought it strange there was no welcoming light in the porch – Mum or Dad always turned it on as the last light faded from the winter sky. I let myself in, hung up my coat and listened. An eerie silence. The door to the small lounge stood open, revealing a pool of light from the standard lamp and the black television screen. I went through to the breakfast room to find it in darkness, the kitchen too. This was very unusual. I couldn't ever remember coming home to an empty house in the evening. I searched for a note – there wasn't one. I felt the tea pot – it was cold. What did this mean? Some sort of emergency and they'd had to leave in a hurry? Anxious thoughts gnawed at the edges of my mind but refused to form themselves. The melancholy wind whistled down the chimney exaggerating the cold emptiness I felt deep inside. Tonight of all nights I needed the warmth and normality of my family around me.

I made a pot of tea, hoping Mum and Dad would soon be home to share it with me. I poured myself a cup, put the cosy on the pot, and took it along to the big dining room. Reflections of the multi-coloured Christmas tree lights sparkled on the window and the street lamp shone into the room. The tree looked forlorn with no presents beneath it now and the happy memory of Christmas morning faded into one of Ron and me sitting on the settee, tapping our feet to the music from the hi-fi. How I wished he was here with me now! I longed for his closeness and his smile and to believe he still wanted me. I wondered how long it would be before I heard from him. The last four days felt more like four weeks. All I asked was a phone call to show he was thinking of me but instead I was left with my head full of doubts.

I sipped the hot tea, a small comfort on this bleak night. It felt strange to sit in here on my own with no purpose but to wait for the family, so I lifted the lid of the piano. There was no one to hear if I made a mistake except the bronze bust of Beethoven that sat atop the piano, glowering down on me. This added to the voices in my head berating me for not continuing with my lessons. I had begged Dad to teach me, but after a few attempts he said he couldn't demonstrate the finer details, so he had sent me to the stuffy Miss Faulkner with her tight grey curls and turned-up nose. I only stuck it for a year.

I began to play the only tune I had learned by heart – a waltz Dad had taught me called Valsette – but it sounded hollow and sad so I closed the lid. Moving across to the hi-fi, I flipped through the records, but to listen to music on my own in my present mood held little appeal.

The sound of a car made me rush to the window. Headlights shone down the road and came to a stop outside the house. I watched Dad slide out of the Anglia and pull the front seat forward for my sister and brother to jump out. Mum followed. They all looked happy and I was relieved that nothing untoward had happened.

I rushed to open the door.

'Hello, love,' said Dad.

'Where were you?'

'At the pictures,' frowned Mum, 'we took Herbie to see *Thunderbirds Are Go*, but I got the showing times wrong. I'm so sorry we weren't here. I couldn't let you know.'

'That's OK. I've made some tea. I hope it's still hot.'

'Oh, lovely, just what I could do with.' Mum went through to the breakfast room with Louise and Herbie, while I followed Dad into the small lounge.

'Was the film any good?' I asked.

A half smile. 'It was all right. Herbie liked it.' He sat down on the settee to remove his shoes and glanced up at me. 'You out tonight, love?'

I shook my head and swallowed hard.

'What? New Years' Eve?'

'To tell the truth, I'm a bit tired.'

'Everything all right?'

I nodded and pressed my lips together.

'You sure? How's Ron lately?'

It was no good; at the sound of his name I hung my head. Dad stood up and put his arm round me. I snuggled into his cosy jumper and breathed in the familiar smell of him. He stroked my hair and I was reminded of Ron doing the same. Hot tears pricked my eyes.

'You can always talk to me, you know.'

'Thanks Dad. I'll be OK.'

MONDAY 2 JANUARY 1967

Marie had arranged to meet me outside the Black Prince. Anything was better than sitting indoors waiting for the phone to ring, but she was late again. I stamped my icy feet to force the blood back into them, then someone tapped me on the shoulder. I spun round.

'Hello, fancy seeing you here!'

I was so happy to see Ron that I couldn't berate him for not getting in touch. 'I was waiting for Marie but it doesn't look like she's coming.'

'D' you want to hang on for a while, see if she turns up?'

I looked at my watch. 'I don't think so. She's never usually this late.'

We went through the usual procedure of paying for our entry to the jazz club. I wondered if he'd tell me why he hadn't rung, but I didn't dare ask. I was just happy to be with him.

The music during the break included *Stop, in the Name of Love* by The Supremes. I thought it very fitting. At the end of the evening I asked Ron if he'd like to come back to the house for a cup of coffee. To my surprise, he accepted.

We sat alone in the kitchen – Ron on the rocking chair, me on the stool – under the glare of the strip light that hummed in the awkward silence. Smudge came in and jumped on Ron's lap, breaking the tension between us. I watched his hands caressing the cat and wished he could be more intimate with me. I made the coffee under his watchful eye, wondering all the while what he was going to tell me. He'd been distant all evening. I handed him his cup of coffee. He stared into it. The sound of Smudge's purring filled the room.

'I'm sorry I've been messing you about,' he began. 'It's just...' He swallowed, tried again. 'It's just... I feel things are getting too serious between us and I'm not ready to settle down. I like my freedom too much.'

I sat down with my coffee, a jumble of words flying round my head. I knew he wouldn't believe me if I told him I had never thought of marriage – I wasn't ready for that. I just wanted him in my life.

'You've got me all wrong,' I began. 'It's not like that.' THINK... THINK, for God's sake! 'What if we didn't see each other quite so often, treat it more...casually?'

He brightened. 'OK,' took a gulp of coffee and sighed, 'but I feel I ought to come clean with you.'

My coffee began to ripple on the surface.

'I've been out with other girls, but nothing serious. Don't look at me like that. I only took Brenda out once, and Jean a couple of times.'

Funny, had I missed these names before? Hadn't I listened? 'Oh, so what about me?'

'Well... I like you a heck of a lot. You definitely come first.'

Was this supposed to make me feel better? Act as some sort of cushion? I was dumbfounded.

Another hush fell on the room. I wanted to ask when I'd see him again but was afraid of the answer.

He checked his watch and started to get up but Smudge dug her claws into his leg. He chuckled and tried to extricate himself. 'Come on, puss. I've gotta catch my train.'

Smudge meowed loudly, on my behalf it seemed. I reluctantly unhooked her claws from his trousers, trying not to pull the threads, and put her on the floor.

I walked Ron to the front door. A quick kiss goodbye then I watched him hurry down the path, wrapping his scarf round his neck. He waved from the gate and shouted, 'I'll phone you.'

SATURDAY 28 FEBRUARY 1987

An air mail letter with Australian stamps fell on the door mat. I rushed to pick it up and hid it under the sofa cushion before Mal or Grace could see it. I exercised my restraint for a whole hour until Mal went out to steam clean a car, something he'd recently taken to in his spare time, and Grace went to Cambridge with friends for the day.

I sat gazing at the letter in my lap, running my finger over Ron's handwriting, the closest I had come to him in twenty years. A sensation ran up my arm and plucked at a string in my chest. I luxuriated in the delicious moment then finally opened the envelope to reveal a belated birthday card, a letter and two photos of Ron taken on his fortieth birthday. In one photo he was holding a cigarette and a can of Foster's. In the other he was smiling straight at the camera while thrusting a knife into his birthday cake. I stared at the images, wanting to imprint them on my memory. Ron still had the same smile but his face was rounder and his hair darker. Of course, it was obvious he wouldn't look the same as I remembered after twenty years. But who was the tanned, dark-haired girl in the background? I wasn't sure what he was trying to tell me.

'G'day mate,

It is really great to be hearing from you again, talk about a surprise.

I have got so much to talk about, it would take the whole of this writing pad, and as you can see, I'm not that used to writing, using the phone is much easier or better still, as we say down here, ' an eyeball to eyeball in depth verbal' is so much better.

The last option is not far off, for I am coming back to England for April and that is only six weeks away from writing this letter.

20 years. What a long time; so much done, a lot of miles travelled, and plenty of tales to tell. One day I might write a book. I bet you have a lot to talk about in your 20 years? It's a long time since The Black Prince.

At the moment I am snatching a few minutes at work to write this letter, so at this stage it will have to be short but I will write a much more detailed one when I have more time.

I am flying back from Sydney March 28th.

Please write back and do take care, see you in April.

       Love

       Ron.

PS Happy Belated Birthday

PPS The photographs are the state of yours truly at the ripe old age of 40.'

A storm of emotion broke over me; he'd written *love*.

I hid Ron's letter, photos and card in my dressing table drawer along with my horoscope from the *Daily Express* on 30 January. 'IF IT'S YOUR BIRTHDAY TODAY – UPHEAVALS likely; it seems that you will be taking the initiative to bring them about. You'll be taking your destiny into your own hands in the year ahead.'

I started to daydream about how and where I would meet Ron and walked around with a smile on my face all day. So he was expecting us to meet six weeks' time! However did it come to this?

In the evening I took myself to the little Priory cinema in Royston to see Paul Hogan in *Crocodile Dundee*. I felt closer to Ron and imagined us watching it together, laughing at the same jokes.

MONDAY 2 MARCH 1987

I'd had a very busy day driving around the villages to different clients, but my last appointment at four-thirty had been cancelled, so I took the opportunity to go round and see Shirley who lived on the council estate. She was a client who'd become my confidante since hearing my news from Australia and I knew she would want to hear the latest. I'd kept Ron's letter to myself all weekend but now I had to tell somebody or I would burst.

Shirley was older than me and she'd had a roller-coaster life. Married at sixteen against her parents' wishes, she'd had two daughters in quick succession. She'd divorced her husband after ten years and married an attractive man much younger than herself and had another two children by him. As her second husband could never hold down a job for long, Shirley was forced to work all hours while her mum looked after the children. But Shirley always made time for me.

We sat opposite one another like a couple of excited teenagers. She held my letter on her lap and looked at me.

'You sure you don't mind me reading it, Julie?'

'Of course not.'

'But it's personal.'

'I don't mind, really. Go on!'

A beaming smile spread across her face as she examined the photos. 'Oh, I do think he's nice, Julie. How do you feel about him now?'

'Excited...but it'll be strange seeing him again after all these years.'

Shirley's eyes bore into mine. 'Won't it just. Who'd have thought?'

'I know. I still can't believe it.'

'Ha, do you think you'll be able to wait till the twenty-eighth?'

'I'll just have to, won't I?'

We discussed what would happen if Ron sent more letters. Shirley offered to have them sent to her address – in case Mal discovered them – like using her as a box number. I had never done anything so devious but I considered this precaution necessary.

In the weeks that followed, I drove around the country lanes to my clients and imagined how Ron felt and what he was doing in Australia. Although he was the other side of the world his spirit was always at my shoulder. I had bought a copy of Andrew Lloyd Webber's new musical *The Phantom of the Opera* and almost wore out the tape listening to it in the car. It was deliciously poignant and I imagined Ron and myself in the starring roles. I bought an atlas and noted all the places in New South Wales Ron had told me about, trying to familiarise myself with the places he'd worked – Brisbane, Canberra, Wagga Wagga. I soaked it all up, everything to do with Australia.

TUESDAY 31 MARCH 1987

Ron's plane had landed at 5.15pm on Saturday. It was a gloomy day but at that precise moment, just for a few seconds, the sun shone like an omen.

I now felt anxious knowing Ron was in Petersfield with his parents. We had tentatively arranged to meet in London tomorrow but I was becoming increasingly nervous at the thought of seeing him again.

At lunchtime I came in from my morning's work to the phone ringing.

'Julie?'

'Yes?'

'It's me, Ron. Well, I'm here. Gee, I tell you, after twenty-four hours on that plane all I wanted was a shower and get my head down! How are you?'

I gripped the receiver a little too tightly. 'I'm fine.'

'Good. All set for tomorrow?'

'I think so.'

'Look, do you think you can you meet me at Trafalgar Square at eleven o'clock?'

'OK. I think I can get away in time.'

'Great. I'm really looking forward to seeing you again.'

'Yeah, me too.'

He'd taken a huge chance phoning my home number. Luckily I was on my own but what if Mal or Grace had been home?

PART TWO

WEDNESDAY 1 APRIL 1987

It's years since I've travelled by train. They are now very different and I'm not entirely sure they're an improvement on the old diesels with their substantial carriages and fuzzy seats.

Wiping my sweaty palms, I close my eyes and try to relax. Again, Ron's image of twenty years ago flashes before me – his blond hair, cheeky smile and the confident swagger in his walk. It's so clear it could be yesterday.

But will I recognise him now? Will he recognise me? How will I feel? Should I be doing this? And is he feeling as nervous as me? I have waited so long for this day but now it's here I feel incredibly disloyal. Although my marriage is stale I have never been unfaithful. I am a stranger to myself; I hardly know what I'm doing.

I never thought life with Mal would become so boring; he wasn't like that when I met him. We were always out in the evenings and thought nothing of hopping up to London or down to Margate, getting home at two in the morning. But now he never wants to go anywhere except the pub.

The train pulls in to Kings Cross and I feel curiously detached, as if I'm looking down on myself. I nervously consult the underground map on the wall to make sure I know where I'm heading.

My heels echo on the stone steps down to the platform. Memories flood in with the metallic smell and oppressive air. Somewhere far off the hollow sound of a train rattles in the tunnel and within seconds my tube screeches into the station. I am cast back to 1966; I am travelling with Ron, his face smiling back at me.

The sight of my reflection in the window brings me up sharp. My Princess Diana hairstyle looks good, but will Ron like what he sees? I remember his remark years ago when I told him I was thinking of having my hair cut: "Don't you dare! I like your long blond hair."

At Charing Cross I rush up the steps and into the spring sunshine. The air is intoxicating, electric. I can't quite believe I'm here. The pigeons flap their wings and part like the Red Sea, heralding my grand entrance down the wide steps towards Nelson's column. My heart pounds against my ribs and a prickly chill breaks over my body. I stop, take a deep breath and do a complete turn, scanning the scene: efficient-looking business people and mothers with children hurrying about. Will Ron show up? I don't know if I want him to, or whether I want him to stay safely locked in my memory. I could easily turn around and go home.

Too late.

There's a man heading towards me dressed in black trousers and a navy sweatshirt. He's fatter than I expected and his hair darker. Oh God! Shall I go ahead with it or forget the whole thing? But as he saunters towards me, his familiar smile lights up his face I can't help but smile back. Somewhere behind those eyes is the Ron I knew. I'm drawn to him. I can't believe this is actually happening.

'Julie? G'day!'

'Hello.'

His eyes scan me from head to toe. 'Oh, jeez. I was frightened you wouldn't show up!' He chuckles nervously. 'It's so good to see you again.'

'You too.'

'How are you?'

'Fine, thanks.' After all these years I can't think of anything to say. There's no embrace, no contact. I feel shy and awkward like the self-conscious teenager I once was, and over-dressed in my royal blue coat and black high heels.

He looks down at his feet and back at me. 'Listen, I want to go buy myself a case for my automatic camera. I think I can see a camera shop over there,' he says, pointing across the road.

I walk with him. He could be anyone but he's Ron, the name still synonymous with the picture I have in my head.

What am I doing here, this is madness.

I hang back while he approaches the young salesman who rummages on the display stand. Looking very pleased with himself, he hands Ron the ideal item.

'You've just sold yourself a camera case, young man,' says Ron, and I get the feeling he's trying to impress me with his attitude. The transaction complete, I turn towards the door.

Ron catches up with me, eagerly, as if he's trying to grasp a mirage. 'Would you like to go with me to Bungee's for old times' sake?' He sounds like a character from a Western, but I agree to go.

It's a long walk. I feel out of step and out of time. He stops, tries to get his bearings and studies the A-Z. 'Er, I think I know, round the corner from The Mousetrap.'

Disappointment tugs at me – he used to be so good at this.

When we finally reach Bungee's it hasn't changed; it's still as shabby as it was twenty years ago and I'm reminded of the one and only time he brought me here. I try to ignore the stale cigarette smoke hanging in the air, and the grimy windows that allow snatches of sunlight to pick out the sticky rings on the dark tables. He sits opposite me, hands me a menu and I'm reminded of La Barcia and the chicken curry. A scruffy woman with lank hair swings out from behind the beaded curtain and takes our order: Spaghetti Bolognese and a glass of lager each – Foster's of course.

I try to ignore the surroundings and hand him my little red tartan diary to read, open at September 12th 1966. Its spotted brown pages held in place with Sellotape turned crisp with age. One page tries to escape; he catches it before it flutters to the floor and gently replaces it, glances at me and reads on.

The lager is plonked in front of us. Ron takes a gulp without looking up, engrossed in the diary.

He carefully hands back the precious material and fixes my attention with his intense gaze. 'I never realised how much I hurt you. Whatever happens, I won't do that again,' he says with conviction.

We eat in silence. He scrapes up the last of the oily meal and downs his lager. I leave half of mine. He wants to go to Chiswick Park to change his return plane ticket. I am swept along by his enthusiasm but I'm unaccustomed to walking very far in high heels and my back is protesting. Again I notice he has to consult the underground map for directions. But the more I listen to him, the more the familiar Hampshire accent surfaces and the years begin to roll back.

Ron successfully changes his ticket to a later date and finally accompanies me back to Kings Cross, only to see my train disappearing into the distance. Panic seizes me – I can't afford be late home – they'll ask questions.

He offers to wait with me on platform nine for the next train. I'm surprised by his concern and try to read his expression. Memories of him waiting with me on Charing Cross station tug at my heartstrings and it saddens me that he makes no reference to them. It's not at all how I expected it to be. There's still no physical contact and I haven't said half what I intended for I'm confused. I don't know how I feel.

'I've really enjoyed being with you today,' he says, searching my face. 'I hope I haven't made you walk too much?'

My back is throbbing but I can't tell him. I can only smile.

'Will they ask where you've been?'

I nod.

'I hope you'll be OK.'

He means it.

My train thunders in and I can't wait to board it. We hurriedly say our goodbyes and as I dart towards the carriage I hear him say he'll ring me tomorrow.

The train stops at nearly every station and I worry all the way to Royston. Finally I jump in my car and drive home, rehearsing all the while what I'm going to say if the need arises.

I park on the drive and brace myself; if only I'd worn jeans.

As I expected, Grace is already indoors doing her homework on the living room floor. Soot sitting next to her, purring. He nuzzles her blonde hair. She turns her head and looks me up and down. 'Where have you been all dressed up?'

My heart drops into my stomach. But I already have something worked out: my mum was admitted to hospital today for a hysterectomy. 'Oh, just went to London for the day.'

'What for?'

'I don't know, really. I suppose I'm a bit worried about Nanna.'

'Oh,' she nods, and goes back to her work. Already I feel guilty. 'Dad's been in… he's gone out to do a car.'

Oh, no! He'll surely want to know where I've been when he comes back. Trying to act as casually as possible, I ask, 'How long will he be? Did he say?'

Grace shakes her head and goes back to her books. I've got nothing planned for dinner, either. It's all going wrong.

Upstairs I change into my jeans and jumper and rehearse how to wriggle out of the inevitable questions.

Mal comes in and I give him the same explanation I gave Grace. He's unusually sympathetic which makes me feel even guiltier. When I tell him about my aching back he even massages it for me while I lie on the floor. This isn't like him; it's as if he's competing for my affections.

'I thought I'd get that car done tonight, seeing as I've got to be here for the secondary double-glazing tomorrow.'

Oh, God! I've forgotten all about that too, and Ron's going to phone tomorrow! I hope he thinks on his feet and says he's dialled a wrong number. No way can I warn him.

THURSDAY 2 APRIL 1987

I shampoo and set my three old ladies at Ashwell who all live in the same road. While I have one under the drier I start the next and so on. They all ask what I did on my day off and I long to be able to tell them. Overnight, the experience has grown into a delicious adventure and heightened my feelings.

When I come back for lunch, all the windows and doors are open and there are strips of metal and wood strewn all over the living room floor. Mal doesn't waste any time in telling me there's been a 'funny' phone call.

I cringe inwardly and try to act vague. 'Oh? Was there?'

Mal nods and watches my expression. It's a close call. I will have to guard against anything like this happening in the future.

Mal goes out for a Chinese take-away in the evening. While Grace is round at Claire's I take the opportunity to phone Ron's mum but he's not there. We exchange pleasantries – Lottie still sounds the same and I'm instantly reminded of the last time I saw her, standing in her hallway saying goodbye. I tell her I'll phone Ron tomorrow morning from Pauline's – another client who's become very interested in my news. I only hope she'll be sympathetic to my needs.

FRIDAY 3 APRIL 1987

When I was subdued with Mal this morning he put it down to the tenth anniversary today of Dad's death, and Mum in hospital. But I feel guilty, even though all I did was to meet an old boyfriend for 'old times' sake'.

I wonder if it'll go any further.

Pauline listens intently while I tell her what's been happening. She's a woman of the world – twice married and divorced and a former high-ranking officer in the army. She gives me permission to confide in her and I ring Lottie. I give her Pauline's number and she gets Ron to call me back.

'Julie?'

'Yeah, it's me.'

'Oh, mate! That was a close one yesterday!'

'I know, I'm sorry. I completely forgot all about the double glazing being done. Mal had to take time off to see them in.'

'Silly bugger! We've got to be more careful in future.'

So he's expecting this to develop.

'I know. You'll have to use this number then Pauline can pass on any messages when I'm not here.'

'Doesn't she mind?'

'No, she knows all about you!'

I hear a slight chuckle. 'Still going to your mum's tomorrow?'

'Yeah.'

'I'll be there. I've got an aunt at Herne Bay – might look her up, too.'

I replace the receiver and squash my twinge of anxiety.

SATURDAY 4 APRIL 1987

These past few days I've been finding it difficult to keep up the pretence that everything's normal and now I relish the thought of getting away. I need to see Mum and check the operation went according to plan and that she's OK. Last night, Mal took Grace to London to stay with his parents for the weekend – a regular occurrence since we moved four years ago. This frees me from the niggling guilt of not being with her.

The drive down to Margate in my Indian Red Nova saloon clears my head and I'm able to think more rationally: I can't afford to make any hasty decisions where Ron is concerned.

I enjoy driving.

My mind runs back to January 1967. After we agreed to keep our relationship more casual, Ron and I saw much less of one another. I continued to go to the Black Prince hoping that by some miracle of telepathy he'd be there, but he rarely was. Marie invited me to join her youth club but all the boys there were too young for me.

I had been learning to drive since the previous August. One evening in January, when I had been unable to concentrate, my driving instructor asked, 'How's your boyfriend, Julie?' The effect of Ron's absence had been that obvious.

I eventually passed my test on the second attempt, five days before my eighteenth birthday, a deadline I had set myself. Not being able to afford a car of my own, Dad agreed to let me drive his Warwick Green Anglia 100e. This was a much greater privilege than using his hi-fi and the burden of responsibility weighed heavily on me – the car was ten years old but Dad kept it in showroom condition.

On the 15th February Marie and I had spent a pleasant afternoon exploring Lullingstone Roman Villa, and afterwards we stopped at Eynsford, a pretty little village near Sevenoaks with a stream and a tea shop that Mum used to take us to in the holidays.

Marie had been in high spirits and burst into song on the way home. Then she suggested we stop off at Greenhithe and call in on Diana, an old convent-school friend of hers. I had little in common with Diana and felt uncomfortable as they laughed and joked together excluding me. They were oblivious of the time and I grew anxious that I should have been home an hour ago.

'We ought to go – Mum'll wonder where I've got to,' I said.

Marie screwed up her nose. 'Oh, all right, then. Go and give her a ring. Tell her you'll be home in half an hour.'

They continued giggling like two schoolgirls while I picked up the phone and told Mum I'd be home at seven-thirty.

Marie knew the area better than me so I let her direct me down the dark country lanes. 'If you go down here we can get out to the A2. It'll be quicker.'

The A2 was the main arterial road from the Kent coast to London and very busy, even in those days. It began to rain as we sat at the junction, waiting for a break in the traffic to turn right, headlamps glaring towards us. Marie kept a watch on the traffic from the left while I watched from the right. It seemed we were waiting a long time and I was getting impatient.

All of a sudden, Marie shouted, 'Now! Go now!'

Without another glance to check the traffic from the right, I took her advice and pulled out onto the main road. The next thing I saw was a pair of headlamps crashing into my right side, the unreal sound of crunching metal and shattering glass. The driver's door was ripped away. Wind and rain gushed in. The car started to spin but I couldn't think how to stop it.

Marie shouted, 'Quick! Jump! Jump out! This side!'

My mind was a blank. This wasn't happening, it was a bad dream.

I was suddenly in a heap in the middle of the road with pairs of headlamps looming towards me.

This is it; I'm going to die.

Two men rushed to my aid. 'Can you stand?' one of them asked.

'I don't know.'

I scrambled to my feet but a terrific pain shot through my right hip and I realised I couldn't walk. They picked me up and helped me to the grass verge and told me an ambulance was on its way. I looked across at Marie – her face was covered in cuts. I looked down at my pale blue anorak smeared with blood.

Is it Marie's?

I looked around and noticed the car had come to rest nose-first in the hedge that lined the grass verge.

Dad will kill me.

The ambulance arrived with blue lights flashing. Marie was lifted onto a stretcher and into the vehicle. They helped me in and I sat with the white-coated attendants wishing I could wake up from the nightmare. The driver of the van that had collided with us was sitting further down in the ambulance, a bloodied handkerchief held to his nose. He looked accusingly at me. With loud bells ringing we were rushed to West Hill hospital in Dartford. As the ambulance veered into the hospital entrance I put out my right leg to steady myself and a terrific pain shot through me.

What have I done?

While I lay on a hospital trolley in the corridor, waiting to go to X-ray, a young police officer asked me to make a statement and to give him all the details of the accident. I was surprisingly lucid and told him exactly what had happened.

I didn't know where Marie was. When I asked, I was told she'd been admitted to a ward.

The X-rays revealed I had a fractured right acetabulum – the socket of the ball and socket joint of the hip. I remembered this from my biology lessons at school and even chatted with the hospital staff, reeling off the bones of the body. My hand had a gash in it but wasn't broken. They put three big stitches in it but I hardly noticed. Eventually, lying flat on my back, I was admitted to the ward where Mum and Dad were waiting with concerned faces. Dad wanted all the details for the insurance so I drew him a diagram.

Mum watched and listened, then said, 'Oh, dear. I think I'm going to be sick,' and left the ward.

They must have stayed with me for an hour then Mum asked if I wanted her to telephone Ron.

'Yes,' I said, 'I think he should know.'

'All right, I'll ring him tomorrow. Try and get some sleep now.'

Will Ron care, and will he come and visit me?

It was a very long and painful night.

MONDAY 20 FEBRUARY 1967

There was no remedy for a fractured pelvis – they couldn't plaster it in that awkward place – I just had to wait for it to mend. Whenever I tried to sit up the pain beat me back, so I had to be fed like a baby. Added to this was the indignity of the bed pans and the bed-baths. I hadn't had anyone to wash me 'down there' since I was a toddler. The ward was full of old women with fractures who had been there for weeks and who screamed for the nurses every night.

I felt very lonely.

I had been in hospital five days when Mum told me that Ron would be coming to see me. On the one hand I couldn't wait, but on the other, I didn't want him to see me like this. I asked one of the nurses to take out my powder compact from the locker so I could apply some make-up. Not an easy task whilst lying down – gravity dictated that bits of make-up fell onto my face.

I lay with my eyes fixed on the clock above the double doors. At seven-thirty they suddenly burst open and the visitors poured in. But no Ron. Another twenty minutes dragged by, then I saw his breezy smile coming towards me.

'Gee, sorry I'm late. What a dead 'n' alive place Dartford is!'

His eyes scanned my vulnerable body clad only in a pink nylon nightie, the sheets pushed down to my waist. He handed me a box of Black Magic chocolates and a get-well card; but I felt helpless when I couldn't reach the locker. I put them on the bed and managed a smile.

He sat awkwardly at my bedside. His grey eyes crinkled. 'I still haven't seen you in that royal blue nightie.'

If he was trying to make me feel better it didn't work. Oh, how I wished I could see him under different circumstances! He talked, mainly about work, but I felt so proud to have him there. I kept glancing at the clock, willing the hands to stand still. He asked what had happened to Marie; I hadn't seen her since the night of the accident.

'She's in another ward; a few cuts on her face and mild concussion, but she's fine apart from that.'

If she can walk, why hasn't she been to see me?

He was going to see if he could find her but I gripped his hand – I wanted him to stay with me.

At eight thirty the bell rang signalling the end of visiting time. I ached for him to stay. He leaned over and kissed me goodbye. 'I'll try and get over next Sunday. Look after yourself.'

I watched him walk through the doors and wished away the hours and days until I saw him again.

Two young Irish nurses came to make me more comfortable.

'Was that your boyfriend, Julie?' asked one.

I nodded.

She winked. 'Very nice! Very nice indeed!'

*

The roads have changed dramatically since 1967; more motorways now. I'm making good time. The M11 wasn't too busy. As I drive up to the barrier on the Dartford crossing I hand the toll money to the attendant, put my Nova in first gear and accelerate onto to the M2.

My mind slips back to that Sunday in West Hill hospital.

3 o'clock and my spirits sank when I saw Mum walking into the ward instead of Ron. He'd managed to get a message to her to say he couldn't make it, but I was devastated. The thought of his visit was the only thing that had kept me from plummeting into the depths of depression.

Mum frowned. 'How are you feeling?' She sat on the chair next to my bed and searched my expression.

'I'm all right, just very bored not being able to do anything.'

'Are you sleeping?'

I nodded. That was all I was doing. I craved oblivion but the reality when I awoke was even more acute.

'Are you getting enough to eat? I've brought you some grapes. Look, I'll put them on your locker.'

'Thanks.' I'd lost what appetite I had. All I wanted was for Ron to bring his smile to my bedside but I knew I'd have to wait another week at least.

The following Wednesday I was transferred to Joyce Green hospital. By now I could sit up in a chair for short spells. But the next day I suffered a set-back in my recovery – I had developed a deep vein thrombosis in my left leg through being stuck in one position for so long. I didn't know which pain was worse – the fracture in my right hip or the DVT. When it was first discovered the doctors and nurses were running about in a panic. Apparently, it was very dangerous if the clot reached my heart – I was put on tablets to thin the blood and every day from then on I had blood taken. The tops of my legs were like pin cushions.

Ron came to visit me on the Sunday. I was even more excited than when he visited me in West Hill. The thought of having him to myself for a whole Sunday afternoon filled me up. Of course, I wanted to look my best, so I had asked one of the nurses to wash my hair. This operation took two of them. They pulled the mattress down at the foot end to create a space to put a bowl of water on the bed springs at the head. Lying on the mattress, one nurse supported my head over the bowl while the other washed my hair; like a backwash. It was a bit uncomfortable but it felt so good to have warm water poured through my hair – I hadn't had it washed for over two weeks. Mum had brought my rollers in the day before and I managed to sit up long enough to set my hair. One of the nurses helped me to dry it. I applied some make-up and I began to feel more like myself.

Mum came to see me first – I think she did this in case Ron didn't turn up – and she remarked how much better I looked. I kept a watchful eye on the clock all the time she was there, unable to concentrate on anything but Ron's visit. When he eventually arrived Mum left us together and I was so happy I wanted to shout, Look everyone, Ron's come to see me!

He pulled up a chair next to my bed, placed a box of Black Magic next to me and kissed my cheek. 'You look much better than the last time I saw you. Now you're sitting up I'll be able to tell Lottie and Jack – they've been very concerned.'

I was gratified by this and somewhere in the distance a little light was beginning to shine – as soon as I was able to walk I'd be able to go to Petersfield again. Spring was just around the corner, then summer and all the lovely events that I imagined taking place. Drives around the countryside with Ron, boating on the lake...

'Thanks for these,' I said, patting the chocolates. 'The food in here is pretty grim.'

'If I'd known I'd have brought you a meat pie or something!'

Oh how I loved him! But time had wings and after forty-five minutes the bell rang signalling the end of visiting time.

'Gee, where does the time go?' Ron patted my hand. 'Suppose I better go. Listen, I'll write, OK? I'll send the letters to your mum.'

I nodded. I was glowing. Somehow I knew this time he would keep to his word.

These letters were more regular than I dared hope, sometimes two a week. I read and re-read them and kept them under my pillow.

Marie had finally come to see me the day before she went home from West Hill hospital. There were a couple of stitches in her forehead and I was relieved her injuries weren't more serious. But she complained of the car door coming back on her leg the night of the accident and I felt this was rather insensitive of her. She knew how bad my injury was and later Mum told her about the DVT which meant my stay in hospital was lengthened to four weeks. She came to Joyce Green to see me a couple of times with other girls from work but I felt our friendship had suffered as a result of the accident.

The day I came home the sun shone and as I was wheeled along in a wheelchair to the ambulance I realised how long I'd been cooped up; I was unaccustomed to the fresh air in my hair, on my skin. A month had passed and the world seemed a very different place to when I was admitted to West Hill. I had mastered the art of walking with crutches and was advised to stay off work for three months. I progressed to two walking sticks, then one stick, and eventually attended out-patients at West Hill for physiotherapy twice a week.

Ron's letters gradually became less frequent and after the last one I realised I wouldn't be getting any more. I was in a terrible state; weeks of lying awake at night, of hurt, confusion and longing. Then, one morning when I was getting ready to go to West Hill, a letter came addressed to Mum in Ron's handwriting.

I watched her open the envelope; she looked bemused. Ron had written two letters; on the folded one: 'Please give this to Julie at the right time.'

She held it out to me. 'Here. I suppose you ought to have this.'

My hand trembled, as if it would burn me if I touched it.

Dear Julie,

I'm sorry I haven't written for some time, but the truth is I've got another job back in my old home town and I feel it would be rather difficult for us to continue to see each other. Also, I have met another girl here. Her name is Jane and we get on very well together. I'm sorry to break it to you like this but I didn't know what else to do. I hope you understand. If I'm ever up your way I'll look you up.

Look after yourself.

Ron.

PS I hope you are continuing to make good progress.

I was stunned. Then hurt. Then angry. With shaking hands I put the letter back in its envelope and looked at Mum.

'Now,' she said, 'Don't do anything silly – he's not worth it.'

'Huh! I'm not about to land myself back in hospital when I've only just come out!'

I held my head up and walked with my stick to the bus stop, trying to focus on how I was walking instead of all the times we had kissed under the moonlight, by the street lamp, within sight of the church...

On the bus, I remembered all the letters he'd sent me. He'd even sent me an Easter card with a picture of daffodils beside a waterfall, and asked if I'd like to go down for Whitsun. Of course, that was out of the question now.

I swallowed down the lump I had been stifling, held my head high, entered the outpatients' department and put Ron from my mind. All that mattered now was getting back to normal.

*

I look at the speedometer – I'm doing 90 and the last thing I need is to get stopped for speeding. I ease off the juice but going slower on motorways always has a soporific effect on me and I go back to 1967 in my mind.

I saw Ron once more in the summer of that year. I went unsuspectingly to answer the door one Sunday afternoon and was knocked sideways to see him standing there larger than life. He told me he'd been to Forest Hill to see an aunt and thought he'd pop in on his way through. I stood to one side to let him in, but I was unsure what he wanted from me. I felt a mess – my hair (now cut short by Marie in the Twiggy style) was in need of a wash. I was also very conscious of the thick support stocking on my left leg. The family were sitting in the garden but Dad must have heard the knock and came in to see who it was.

His eyes flashed at Ron. 'What do you mean by coming here upsetting Julie? I think you've got a nerve...'

But Ron had such a way with him that he won Dad round. 'I'm sorry, I truly am but I was in the area and couldn't pass by without knocking.'

'All right. You'd better come though.'

I followed them through to the garden and Ron ended up sitting with us, chatting like a long-lost relation.

Mum made him welcome and asked me to make a fresh pot of tea. I put the kettle on and watched Ron through the kitchen window, sitting in a deck chair on the lawn under the shade of the tulip tree, talking to Mum and Dad.

Why did you come? Don't you know how I feel?

I carried the tea tray into the sun-washed garden, aware of Ron's eyes on me. Louise and Herbie were playing ball on the top lawn, their laughter piercing through the quiet afternoon. I set the tray carefully on the picnic table, poured the tea and tried not to shake as I handed Ron his cup. He thanked me and carried on talking as if I wasn't there. He showed an interest in Dad's Rolex watch and Dad took it off to demonstrate how it worked on motion alone. I watched them, heads together, absorbed in the mechanics and wondered if Ron would finally speak to me.

After an hour he got up to leave. I saw him out to a white Mini with blue wheels parked outside. He sensed I wanted an explanation as to why he'd come but he couldn't look me in the eye.

'I couldn't come all this way without seeing you.'

What do you want from me?

'Are you back at work?'

'Only just – it's tiring having to stand for any length of time,' I said, looking down at my bad leg.

'Yeah, I bet.'

We stood awkwardly by the car. I thought he would've gone by now; I didn't know if I wanted him to or not.

Why did you come?

I jumped in with both feet. 'How's Jane?'

The question hung in the air, waiting.

He looked sheepish. Bit his lip and kicked a stone in the road. 'Er...that's finished. She's moved away.'

He looked directly at me for my reaction. I looked down at my feet and tried not to smile – I found it amusing that someone had given him a taste of his own medicine.

'Remember me to your mum and dad,' I said, at length.

'Yeah, I will. Well, must dash. It's been nice seeing you again, I might see you again sometime. Look after yourself.'

He got in the car and wound down the window, smiled and waved and drove out of my life. With mixed feelings I watched the car disappear and vowed to lock him away in the bottom drawer of my mind.

But on a Wednesday evening in June the following year, Ron turned up again like the proverbial bad penny.

It was now very unusual for me to be home in the evening – my friend Lorna, who had recently joined the salon, and I went out every night to different clubs and pubs and tried to forget about the boys who had left us by the wayside. We had been to Hide's restaurant one lunchtime and I'd told her all about Ron; the whole story. Not long after, Terry, her tall and handsome fiancé of two years, ditched her for someone else. She was devastated; he was her whole world. We now had something in common and went out to drown our sorrows in places like The Vic and Bull at Dartford, The Well Hall at Eltham and The Falcon at Falconwood. But The Black Prince remained our favourite. As well as the jazz club on Mondays, there were great gigs on Sunday evenings with famous names like Gino Washington and the Ram-Jam Band, John Mayall, and The Ferris Wheel. There was always live music or a disco somewhere and we danced many a night away. 'Burning the candle at both ends?' Dad would say with a smile. I don't think Mum approved – she gave me some very disparaging looks.

But on this particular Wednesday evening I had decided to have an early night. I was getting ready for bed, peeling my false eyelashes off, when the telephone rang.

Dad shouted up the stairs, 'Phone for you, Julie!'

I ran down to answer it. Ron was phoning from the Black Prince – he was coming to pick me up and take me down there for a quick drink and said he'd give me a few minutes to get ready. He arrived at ten-thirty. He looked different, but then so did I – I'd had my blonde hair cut in an elfin style and wore super-short mini skirts and chunky heels. We sat in one of the bars but I felt bare and self-conscious without my heavy make-up. He bought me a gin and tonic, my drink of choice, and told me about his new job – a sales rep for Pye Records which took him all over the south of England. He was full of it. In fact he spoke of nothing else. Until: 'Mum and Dad asked to be remembered to you.'

I thought of Lottie and Jack with fondness but didn't think I would ever see them again.

'You courting?'

I nodded. 'I'm going out with a coach driver at the moment – he phones me up at the drop of a hat and asks me to meet the coach at the traffic lights. All the old-age pensioners cheer when I get on! He took me to the Kurzall at Southend last Saturday night and the Sunday before we went to Hastings for the day. The castle is great. Have you been there?'

He shook his head.

'He makes me laugh with all his stories and he has the passengers in stitches. I thought I saw him just then, in that Margo's coach,' I said, pointing out the window.

Ron raised his eyebrows but it happened to be true – I had met Bob at The Falcon one evening, when he'd been acting as a bouncer. Also, I thought Ron had a nerve thinking he could drop into my life whenever he felt like it and take up where he left off. I wanted to prove I was enjoying life without him, didn't want to massage his ego. Part of me didn't like the self-centred person he'd become, but we laughed and joked. He was very up-beat.

'Gee, it really is good to see you again,' he said, searching my face. 'You've changed.'

Of course – you've had something to do with that.

'Time gentlemen, please!' shouted the barman.

Ron drained his glass. 'I'd better get you home.'

We sat in his Mini outside the house. It felt too intimate. Too close. I didn't want to drop my barriers; I had relied on them for too long.

He turned to me. 'I'll give you a ring next time I'm up this way.'

I behaved overly cheerful, gave him a quick kiss on the cheek and got out the car. 'Thanks for the drink.'

'That's OK. So long.' He flashed me a smile, put the car in gear and drove out of my life again.

So, after the two-hour drive on this bright April morning, I pull up outside Mum's little terraced house in Margate and my twenty-six year old brother, Herbie, greets me at the door. He's over six feet tall; an Arnold Schwarzenegger look-alike having been into bodybuilding since he was fifteen. He still lives at home but Louise, our middle sibling, left home shortly after Dad died. Even though I'm twelve years his senior, I have always been quite closer to Herbie. I used to love taking him shopping and on bus journeys when he was little.

Mum's partner, Tom, is at work. Dad died ten years ago and I struggle with my emotions, wondering what he would have made of Tom. There was no one like my dad – he was artistic and charismatic and carried an aura around him. Tom is a porter at the local children's home; very ordinary, but he'll do anything for anybody and is devoted to Mum.

Over a pot of tea, I briefly tell Herbie what's been happening at home and that I'm expecting a phone call. He sits opposite me and searches my face but he's more understanding than I thought he'd be.

'You can use the phone upstairs if you like – it'll be more private.'

'Thanks.'

I sit by the little table on the landing staring at the mixture of dried flowers. The phone rings on cue.

'Julie?'

'Yes.'

'Oh, good! I'm glad I've caught you. I've decided I'm not coming today, it's too risky. I can't put you in that danger. I've been thinking – what if something leaks out in conversation?'

'OK. You're probably right.'

'Listen, I've got a better idea – how about meeting me at Sevenoaks tomorrow?'

'OK...you'll have to let me know where.'

He seems to be going to extraordinary lengths to keep me our meetings secret. Is it necessary?

'Sure. How's your mum?'

'Fine, I think. I'm going to see her soon.'

'OK. Send her my regards. I'll ring again when I know what I'm doing.'

I go with Herbie to see Mum at the hospital in the afternoon. She looks remarkably well for someone who's just undergone a major operation and even manages to walk to the toilet independently, whilst wheeling the intravenous drip alongside her. She smiles at the nurses and tells me how well they are looking after her. I'm relieved. I tell her briefly about my meeting with Ron but she can't remember him.

I spend the rest of the day with Herbie. I wonder how long it'll be before he finds a girl and settles down. He's never been very lucky in his personal life. I tell him about my boring marriage and the story of Ron up to the present day. He listens, taking it all in.

'Look, if you need to talk anytime, don't hesitate to get in touch.'

'Thanks. I didn't know how you'd take it. You and Mal always got on well.'

He shakes his head. 'It's fine, Julie. You know what you have to do. If it's got to that stage with Mal...'

The next day, Ron rings again.

'I'm sorry but I don't think it's a good idea for us to meet tomorrow; it'll be the same scenario as yesterday.'

I agree. 'I know. I've been chewing it over too.'

'Do you think you can meet me at Kings Cross on Wednesday?'

I'm so happy he's said that. 'Yeah, this time I'll make sure I get my act together!'

He chuckles.

WEDNESDAY 8 APRIL 1987

This, I assure myself, is going to be a much better day than last Wednesday. Anticipating more walking, I dress casually in jeans, jumper and flat shoes which won't raise suspicion if I'm a bit late home. But I don't plan on making the same mistake twice.

As I step off the train at King's Cross I'm surprised to see Ron walking towards me with a smile that spreads into a wide grin. I bravely give him a kiss, the first for twenty years. He beams.

I take him to the Trocadero and show him the hologram exhibition. We are both impressed by the amazing 3D pictures that seem to jump out at us. I want to show Ron what I know of London – I brought Grace here only a few weeks ago but now that memory feels compromised. I bury it and concentrate on being with Ron, making the most of our time together. Over coffee we discuss the merits of both London and Sydney. I feel patriotic and protective of my capital city while Ron extols the positive virtues of Sydney – vibrant and alive with new ideas. After all our phone conversations I feel I know him a little better – this allows us to be more open with each other. He speaks of his feelings, something he's never really done before.

'What I don't want to do is hurt you again. I couldn't live with myself if I did.'

I smile inwardly. He's grown up. I like the person he's become and I sense the feeling is mutual. Also, after twenty years, it's unbelievable that we have the same likes and dislikes.

'Have you got a passport?' he asks. 'I would love to show you Sydney.'

I nod enthusiastically but I don't know where all this is leading. He's galloping ahead so fast and I don't know if I'm ready.

The lights of Piccadilly Circus are reflected in the wet pavements and ignoring the dark skies we take photos of one another other under Eros.

'Very appropriate!' he jokes.

While he snaps me I feel like a fashion model being photographed, but deep down I'm aware of my appearance; if only I could've dressed for the occasion. Very aware of the time, we talk as we walk, not wanting to waste a moment. In The Haymarket we hover outside Her Majesty's Theatre gazing at the photos from *The Phantom of the Opera.*

'One day, I'll take you to see it,' he promises.

I don't hold him to it but having imagined Ron and myself in the starring roles so many times, this excites me beyond belief.

Next stop the National Gallery. The security attendant checks our belongings and asks us to leave our umbrellas at reception. We stroll around the halls barely looking at the paintings. As we sit on the couch in the middle of one of the large deserted rooms, the imposing works of art seem to be waiting for an exchanged confidence. He takes my hand and looks at me intently. 'I want to come back to this country; I've got everything to come back for now – you!'

This is all going too fast. I feel dizzy like a child on a roundabout out of control.

'I felt a bit depressed over the weekend,' he said.

'Why? Because you didn't see me?'

He nods.

After only two meetings?

We saunter around Covent Garden, holding hands. There are some street performers strutting their stuff. One of the jugglers is making a mess of his performance, dropping balls left and right. One rolls towards us. Ron picks it up and throws it back to him. He misses and looks pathetic.

Ron shouts, 'Shoot him now and put him out of his misery!'

The crowd laughs. I laugh with them and squeeze Ron's hand. I haven't had so much fun in ages.

He reluctantly accompanies me back to King's Cross. We wait on the platform. He agitatedly looks around then turns me to face him. 'What are you doing next Wednesday?'

'Nothing.'

'Well, you are now!'

The train rolls in and I slip him a folded piece of paper. 'Read it when I've gone.'

He beams and kisses me goodbye. The kiss is different. He's different. He's given me a lot to think about.

The piece of paper contains some lines from *The Phantom of the Opera*:

'Think of me, think of me fondly when we've said goodbye,
Remember me, once in while, please promise me you'll try.'

THURSDAY 9 APRIL 1987

I watch Grace walk down the road to school and close the front door. The phone rings and I wonder how Ron always manages to pick the right time. He sounds elated, restless. 'I couldn't wait till tomorrow when you're at Pauline's. How do you feel?'

'On top of the world!'

'I feel the same. Listen, I've made a decision – I'm going back to Sydney a week early to get things tied up over there, then I'm coming straight back!'

It this really happening?

'Did you read the lines I gave you?'

'Yeah, I've written a reply. I didn't know I was such a bloody poet!'

'See what I do for you?'

'Ha,yeah. I'll give it to you next week.'

FRIDAY 10 APRIL 1987

I'm barely through Pauline's door when her phone rings. She tells me to use the one in her kitchen – it's more private.

'Hi, I've just arrived,' I breathe, my heart pounding.

'You happy?'

'Yes, very.'

'How d'you feel about living down the West Country?'

I feel giddy. 'Anywhere, as long as it's with you!'

'My sentiments exactly. Oh, mate, we've got a lot to do. A lot ahead of us. It's a bit scary.'

'Mm, I know.'

A short pause as he considers this. 'Anyway, I'm sure we'll be OK. I love you.'

Twenty years I've waited to hear those three little words and even now, I can't quite believe it.

'I love you too,' I say, this time without fear of his reaction.

SATURDAY 11 APRIL 1987

I drive down to Mum's again for the weekend. She's almost back to normal although she's been told to take it easy. I make lunch for us all, Herbie, Mum and me. Tom's at work. Herbie and I go to Broadstairs in the afternoon. I spot a shop with a big diagram of a hand outside. On impulse, I step inside. I could never resist a palmist and Olandah has been in the business for years.

It's not really Herbie's scene but he goes along with it and follows me in. Olandah asks us to take a seat on her sofa in her dark and mysterious room, ethereal music tinkling softly in the background and a crystal ball sitting invitingly on her coffee table. Wearing a home knit, Olandah sits in an armchair looking like someone's dear old granny, not a wart in sight. She tells me to hold the crystal ball while she talks to me, then reads from it. I glance at Herbie. He smiles as she starts to tell me about things that have happened in the past – the sign of a good medium.

She then tells me: 'You will be getting good news from abroad, the future is very bright and there will be lots of opportunities. You must take them. You will be going to a celebration party in May and a family wedding in August. I can see a baby...yours... and you will write a book about your life, one day. You will also have a long and happy life. Is there anything you want to ask?'

I take a deep breath. 'There's someone who's come back into my life after twenty years – can you tell me the outcome?'

She studies my face and takes a few moments to compose the answer. 'He's changed a lot; he used to be harem-scarem but now he's settled down. What star sign?'

'Sagittarius.'

She nods. 'Date?'

' The ninth of December.'

'Yours?'

'Aquarius, thirtieth of January.'

She nods again. 'This is a very romantic combination and your birth numbers vibrate perfectly together. He's had you in his thoughts more than he's cared to admit over the years. But by this time next year, everything will have settled down and you will get your wish; leave everything to providence – it will all happen!'

I'm floating. She also tells me that I have five guardian angels to protect me. They could come in very useful.

I turn to Herbie. 'Your turn!'

He smiles his little boy grin. 'Oh, all right, then.'

I watch Olandah study his face and then the crystal ball. She doesn't take as long with him. Maybe she knows how awkward he feels or maybe it's because he hasn't got so much history. But she manages to tell him there is someone for him – a girl he has yet to meet. It will soon happen and they will be very happy. I hope she's right. Herbie hasn't had much luck with women up till now.

MONDAY 13 APRIL 1987

I ponder Olandah's prediction. I can't believe she was so in tune with my thoughts. The phone rings. I rush downstairs to answer it. Luckily, Mal left for work half an hour ago and Grace has gone to school. It's as though Ron knows – as if there's a CCTV camera in our hall. But it's so good to hear his voice that I can't caution him.

'Good weekend?'

'Yeah but I've missed you,' I tell him.

'Yeah, I've missed you too. I was at Lofty's in Bristol at the weekend. He remembers you.'

So Lofty is still in the picture. I wonder if he's changed, too. 'How is he?'

I heard the smile in his voice. 'Still the same old Loft. He's happy – got a nice family and nice house. I found myself wishing that you were there with me.'

'I went to my mum's for the weekend.'

'Oh, yeah? How is she?'

'Well, put it this way, she looked a lot better when I left.'

'Ah, that's what I need – *you* around me. Oh, mate! I'm definitely coming back to England. Won't change my mind; I've got everything to come back for now!'

'I can't believe this is happening.'

There's a short pause at his end, then he blows out a sigh. 'Oh, what are you doing to me? What are we doing to each other? I wish I was seeing you today, tomorrow and Thursday and Friday, Saturday and Sunday! I'm going to get my plane ticket changed. I'll tell you about it when I see you on Wednesday.'

He hasn't asked but assumes we will meet again on my day off. This time we arrange to meet at Tesco's at Baldock. He's worried that my journeys to London will be found out.

Ron has rented a car and says he'll see me in the car park at 1 o'clock. My heart thumps as I put the phone down. I'm so full of energy I could climb Everest.

WEDNESDAY 15 APRIL 1987

Feeling brighter than the sunny morning, I drive to Baldock. I smile at the irony: Mal works for Tesco supermarkets at their head office. He's worked his way up from a Saturday Boy, to having his own sales promotion team and now he's a senior planner.

I first met Mal in December 1968 at his friend Steve's twenty-first birthday party. When Lorna and I arrived at the little terraced house in Peckham, the party was in need of a shake-up – Bill Hailey's *Rock Around the Clock* blaring out.

'What's this rubbish?' said Lorna, and made a dash for the record player. 'Come on, Blue! (Her nickname for me because of my blue eyes) We've gotta do something about this!'

We flipped through the records and found some Diana Ross and Tamla Motown – our favourites. Lorna and I took the floor. The house was heating up, jumping to the beat. The beer and spirits flowed. From the edge of my vision I saw someone watching me. He had a Steve McQueen haircut, grey Tonik suit and Chelsea boots. When he finally asked for a dance, he was smiley and cheerful and told me to call him Mal, *not* Malcolm. During the course of the evening, I became too hot for the long half-wig I was wearing and daringly removed it to reveal my now boyish haircut. I wasn't prepared for his reaction.

'That's better!'

I thought most men preferred long hair.

Shortly after this I made a dash for the bathroom, but the door was locked. I threw up before I could get in there, thoughts of that New Years' Eve party in 1966 surfacing. I kept apologising but no one seemed to care. Then Mal walked me up and down in the freezing, snow-covered street to sober me up. Dressed only in a mini-length waistcoat suit and satin blouse, I was so drunk I didn't feel the cold. I stayed with him into the small hours. He was running people home in his white Vauxhall Cresta, until he finally took me home at four in the morning. I felt safe with him. But Dad was not very pleased with me the next day – staying out all night with someone I'd only just met – but he eventually warmed to Mal. He said he was a 'decent sort'.

On the evening of my twentieth birthday, a few weeks after the party, I was waiting for Mal to pick me up when the phone rang. I naturally thought it was Mal phoning to say he would be late, but instead it was Ron! He rang to wish me happy birthday just as he had the previous year. We briefly caught up with news then I told him I was going out shortly and regretted not being able to talk for longer.

Mal arrived with a huge box of chocolates and a bunch of flowers. He took me out for a drink at a cosy pub in Bexleyheath but I couldn't obliterate Ron from my mind. Mal and I sat by the roaring log fire, chatting, getting to know one another. I told him a little about Ron, but I lied when I said I was over him.

In retrospect, Ron would probably have carried on the tradition of wishing me happy birthday every January, but Dad's workload had been seriously cut and he couldn't afford the upkeep of our five bedroom house anymore. In April 1969 we were forced to move to a three bedroom semi near Bexley station. I never sent Ron our new address. Thinking there was no future in it, I had tried to put him from my mind. I had moved on; by the summer, Mal and I were serious about each other and talking of getting engaged.

Now, dead on 1 o'clock, the sun pierces a cloud as I drive into Tesco's car park. I choose a space well away from the other cars so Ron can spot me. I wait, listening to *The Phantom of the Opera* on the cassette player

His beaming smile is suddenly beside me at the open window.

'Hello, how are you?'

I hurry out of the car. I want to kiss him but there are a lot of people about. 'I'm fine. And you?'

'Yeah, been here since eleven forty-five!'

'Really?'

'Listen, I think it's a better idea if we use my car, in case anyone recognises yours. Can't be too careful.'

'I can take the magnetic Dial-a-Style signs off the doors – it's not a problem.'

He looks around then shakes his head. 'Nah, I'd feel a lot happier if we did this my way.'

'OK.'

I feel rather vulnerable as I sit in the rented blue Morris Marina. Shielding my eyes against the sun, I direct him to The Jester, a sweet old country pub in Ashwell. The three elderly ladies I shampoo and set fortnightly live here, and after Ron's concern, I hope no one spots me. But conversely, I feel so proud, I long to show him off.

We each order a ploughman's and Foster's and make ourselves comfortable. I give Ron my blue hardback diary to read that I've been keeping since our first contact three weeks ago. He smiles at me, takes a gulp of his lager and starts to read it.

He looks up. 'I can't believe this.'

'What?'

'Wait here.'

He plonks his drink down and dashes out to the car. Comes back with an almost identical diary for me to read! My skin tingles when I read his words. After the first meeting: "Met Julie in Trafalgar Square. She is beautiful! We were both a bit guarded..." After the second: "Met Julie in London. God! I love her! I took some good photos of her under Eros. Very apt!" And yesterday he had written, "Meeting Julie tomorrow. Can't wait!" He would never have been this open twenty years ago.

I look up from the diary and he's finished his lunch and drunk his lager. I'm only halfway through mine.

'Is there somewhere we can go, not far from here?' he asks.

I nod. 'Most of this area is pretty.'

'OK. Shall we go?' He looks at my plate. 'Oh, if you've finished, of course.'

'It's fine.'

As we drive around the country lanes, the sun sparkling through the trees, I'm reminded of us doing the same in Petersfield in 1966. I feel renewed. Grace and Mal push into my thoughts. I push them away – I don't want anyone or anything to ruin our afternoon.

We stop off the beaten track – a wooded area providing a cloak for us – and take photos of one another. I can't quite believe he's back in my life after all these years – I want to savour every minute, embed it in my memory. My love for him and the sun warm me in equal measure. All my senses are heightened when he holds my hand.

It feels like only half an hour has passed when Ron reluctantly drives me back to Tesco's. But when I look at my watch it's 3 o'clock.

I grab a basket at Tesco's entrance.

He follows my lead. 'Yeah, I could do with a few things.'

It feels very strange to be together in this domestic situation. At the checkout, I look at Ron's basket – it's full of cans of Foster's and very little else.

He smiles cheekily, 'You can tell I've got my priorities right!'

Afterwards, we go to the café. We both choose Earl Grey tea. He tells me he also likes gin and tonic.

The same as me!

He insists we sit opposite each other. 'I want to be able to see your face, your expression.'

No one has ever said this to me before.

'I think we've got a lot in common,' he smiles, putting his warm hand on mine. Then his mood suddenly changes. He's serious, full of energy. 'I'm flying back to Sydney on Sunday night, 10 o'clock; sell my belongings and come straight back.'

Oh God. It's actually happening.

He looks at me for a reaction but I can only smile.

We finish our tea and go to sit in the Marina. He moves slowly closer, kisses me then looks into my eyes. How I remember that look!

'Now, what you've got to do is act normal. How d' you feel?'

'I don't know.'

He squeezes my hand. 'Tell me in six weeks' time.'

THURSDAY 16 APRIL 1987

At 9am Ron phones me at Pauline's from his brother's business at Portsmouth. I answer it in the kitchen amongst the evidence of the cooking Pauline's been doing for an antiques fair, her new venture. There are remains of half-cooked food all over the worktops, her sink is blocked and flies buzz around. The smell is putrid. I concentrate on Ron's voice and the kitchen recedes into the background. He says he hasn't slept all night for thinking about what he's got to do.

'How do you feel?'

Why does he keep asking me?

'Happy.'

'Me too. I think we've got a battle ahead of us; it won't be easy, but then again, nothing worth having ever is. I'm going to try and get back in six weeks. I want to try and get Australian citizenship, too, so I can go back whenever I want.'

Still the 'I' – this unsettles me. 'I'd like to go with you next time.'

'Ha, yeah, that'd be great.' He starts to chuckle, then the pips go. I hang up. The phone rings again.

'Hello?'

'The money ran out. Sorry.'

There's a pause, then, 'How long have we been together?'

'I've added it up. Thirteen and a half hours, that's all.

'Gee! Haven't we got some great times ahead?'

'We sure have.'

'Anyhow, I've gotta go now – no more change. I'll try and phone before I go back. I love you.'

'Love you too.'

Pauline wants the latest – I give her an update. She smiles but I can't read her thoughts. I could happily talk about Ron all morning but I have to grit my teeth and wash her hair over the filthy sink to which she is oblivious.

GOOD FRIDAY 1987

Mal goes round to Claire's to walk Grace back home. While he's gone, I take the opportunity to ring Ron at his mum's, but he can't talk for long as he's going to dinner at a mate's house.

Why is it so important? Who is this 'mate'?

I put it to the back of my mind and tell him about the barbecue we had this evening. Ron and I discuss different ways of cooking chicken – we're so together on everything.

'I've been to the Isle of Wight today to take the car back. It was gloriously sunny over there.'

'Yes. It was here. I wish I'd been with you.'

'Yeah, so do I... We're having a bit of a get-together tomorrow before I fly back, round Sally's.'

There it is again – that insensitivity.

'A pity I can't be there.'

'Yeah. That's a shame.'

Another pause.

He changes the subject, talks about old original records being worth a lot of money. I tell him I have the original 45 of The Beatles – *I Wanna Hold Your Hand.*

'I love to hold yours!'

I imagine his smile.

'Listen, I'll phone you, 1.15 Sunday lunchtime. Right now I've gotta go.'

'I hope I'm on my own.'

'Yeah, me too. Oh! I forgot to give you my answer to the words you wrote last week. I've written something else, too – you'll be getting it through the post next week sometime.... Oh, I just wanna be *with* you!'

'I know; we've just gotta be patient.'

'Yeah. Talk to you Sunday. Must dash – I'm gonna be late.'

I reluctantly put down the phone and feel very envious of the people he'll be spending time with over the next couple of days.

EASTER SUNDAY 1987

On cue Ron phones as promised. Grace is in the living room so my words are guarded. I want to tell him how much I love him and it'll seem like a lifetime before he comes back, but it's impossible.

He takes the words out of my mouth. 'Whatever happens, I love you and I'll be back as soon as I can. I'd like to be back in four weeks. I've got a lot to do, but you know all of this. I've written you a poem...I'll send it from Australia. I promise you a life you'll never forget...if you know what I mean!'

'I love you,' tumbles out quietly.

Grace rushes past me and up to her bedroom. She closes the door.

I take the opportunity to talk more freely. 'Mal's been very awkward today.'

'Has he? Do you think he suspects anything?'

'I don't know. I hope not.'

A heavy sigh. 'I've got a tear in my eye now, cause I don't wanna go.'

'I know. I don't want you to, either.'

'Be back in four weeks, if not sooner. I promise.'

'I hope so. Have a safe journey. I'll be thinking of you.'

'And you look after yourself. You know what you have to do. See you in four weeks.'

'Bye. Love you.'

Grace went round to Claire's this afternoon and stayed for tea. At 10pm I walk round to collect her. I stand and look up at the star-filled navy sky and imagine Ron somewhere up there in a jumbo jet.

Please God, keep him safe for me and let him come back soon.

A chill runs down my spine, as if my spirit is trying to reach out to his across the immense atmosphere.

EASTER MONDAY 1987

Mal told me this morning that he'd had a terrible dream – something big and grey pulling him out of bed. He wrestled with it. It was all he could do to fight it off and he showed me the bruises on his shoulder to prove it! When he woke up he thought the demon was still in the room; he sensed it at the foot of the bed but couldn't see its face. I can't believe this – it's as if there's a spiritual force trying to part us.

We hang around the house doing jobs that have mounted up: cleaning cars, cutting lawns. I feel detached from my body as if I'm on auto-pilot. The atmosphere is strained all day.

Then, just before we go to bed, Mal sits on the edge of the sofa, his clasped hands on his knees, and looks me straight in the eye. 'Right, what's going on? You got someone else? I know something's wrong cause your character's changed.'

Like a giant tsunami the words gush out before I can think – everything – how I knew Ron twenty years ago, how I got in touch with him and how unbelievable it all is, like something that only happens in books. The earth seems to stop, time suspended. Mal sits wide-eyed, dumbstruck.

A larger than usual gulf has opened up between us. Unspoken words hang in the air.

I am no longer a part of you. We are strangers.

'Right,' he shouts, 'that's it. You'll have to get yourself sorted out and go! You can tell Grace in the morning. And you can phone *him* in Australia and tell him that I know!'

Oh God. What have I done?

I start to shake uncontrollably. An inexplicable force has picked me up, spun me round and dropped me in the same place but on the other side of time. I want to turn back the clock, start again, approach it differently. But too late, the damage has been done. There is no way back.

He turns to me as he opens the door to go to bed. 'I knew this morning – that grey thing – it was warning me.'

What will I do now? Where will I go? What about Grace? What will she think of me?

TUESDAY 21 APRIL 1987

It's still dark when I wake up. It dawns on me that the nightmare is real – I didn't dream it. I stumble downstairs, make a cup of tea and automatically take one up for Mal.

He leans his head on his elbow, rubs a hand over his face. 'Right, I'm going in to work early and when I came back, I wanna talk. In the meantime, you phone Australia, and you tell Grace what's going on.'

I feel like a child being reprimanded.

What will Ron say? Ten hours in front – it'll be evening there. Has he even arrived?

I don't know whether to phone Ron before I tell Grace, or tell Grace before I phone Ron. I pace the living room floor, my stomach in knots.

Mal goes to work without any breakfast.

I hear Grace getting up. It's no good – I'm going to have to tell her first. I don't want her to learn through my conversation with Ron; it's not right. None of it's right. But I brace myself and drag my feet up the stairs. Every step a little nearer to the gulf I must inevitably open up between us.

She's in her school uniform sitting on her bed, sorting out her books. I knock on her open door.

'Can I come in?'

She nods, unsuspecting.

Here goes. 'I've got something to tell you – it's not very nice, I'm afraid.' I take a deep breath. The words trip over themselves and come out clumsily. 'I'm leaving your dad. I've got someone else, but he's not here – he's in Australia.'

An achingly long silence stretches out between us until she manages a solitary, 'Oh.'

I feel as if I'm standing outside myself, watching the scene. Time stretches into infinity before Grace says anything else; she looks down at her hands and starts picking at her nails. I don't know what to do or say; we've grown so apart over the years. I feel awkward and ill equipped to deal with this situation. She swallows then looks up at me with an expression that's difficult to read. Then, in a tiny voice, 'When? When are you going?'

'I don't know, yet. Probably in a month's time.'

'Oh.'

Another uncomfortable silence. I stand rooted to the spot, speechless. I try to edge my way onto her bed, next to her, but she doesn't move over to make room for me so I get up again. I feel a phoney when I put my arm round her. She's unresponsive, like a block of wood.

'It's not that I don't love you,' I venture, 'You must never think that.'

She pulls away from me; my arm drops. A gaping wound has opened up and I can't think of anything to do or say to begin to heal it. I leave her and go downstairs. All I can focus on now is phoning Australia; doing what's expected of me. I stare at the phone. Fear grips me. I know Ron's number even though I've never used it. I start to shake as I pick up the handset and dial 61 for Australia, then the long number. He answers straight away.

'Hello! This is a nice surprise.'

Oh God. If only...

I brace myself for his reaction. My voice shakes. 'I'm sorry, but it's not. Mal knows – he got very awkward last night and I ended up telling him everything. I don't know what to do. He's gone to work but he's coming back at ten, to talk.'

Ron sounds flustered, shocked. 'OK, er... listen, are you all right? He hasn't hurt you has he?'

'No, I'm fine. Bit frightened, that's all.'

'Yeah, I bet.' He blows out a breath. 'What about if you talk to him, try and smooth things over?'

How? The damage has been done.

'I don't know.'

'OK er...Oh, God, this is awful – I'm too far away to *do* anything, that's the trouble.'

'I know.' I can hear him chewing his lip. He sounds really worried, and none too pleased that I've dropped the bombshell.

'Look. Try not to worry too much. I'll ring you later. I love you.'

Grace goes off to school with her rucksack slung over her hunched shoulders, head bowed. I walk about the house, trying to think. I go into overdrive, phone all my customers that are booked in today and cancel their appointments. I tell them something's cropped up. A massive understatement.

10 o'clock dead on the dot, Mal drives up, chucks his keys on the hall table and strides into the living room. I make a pot of tea as if it's a normal day.

The phone rings. I jump.

Mal turns towards the hall. 'Is that *him?* Let me talk to him!'

He snatches the phone. Pushes me back into the living room and closes the door. I walk the floor, wringing my hands. I can't hear what he's saying until he raises his voice, 'Don't you ever come here – if I ever see you I'll cut your fucking head off! Do you realise the grief you've caused?'

He slams the phone down and comes back into the living room, drops down on the sofa with his head in his hands. He looks up and stares blankly into an unknown future. Seconds tick by. He looks at his hands, then at me. 'Look... I can see you're worried; I'm not gonna throw you out, I can't do that.'

I don't feel worthy of his concern. I'd had visions of him throwing me out on the front lawn with my bags round my ears. It was stupid to tell Mal everything last night but I still feel completely detached from him. My concern now is for Ron and how he must be feeling all those miles away, unable to do anything. And poor, poor Grace, at school.

WEDNESDAY 22 APRIL 1987

It's now one whole week since I last saw Ron and I miss him dreadfully. The debilitating sense of foreboding will not leave me but I feel slightly better after spending the night on the chair-bed in the living room. Mal gets up and comes downstairs, makes tea. Hands me one, sits on the sofa and stares at me. His hair is dishevelled, dark circles under his eyes.

He takes a breath. 'Don't do anything silly like trying to find somewhere else to live. If you can't face sleeping with me, have the spare room.' He pauses, looks absently out the window. 'I knew I never had you. I realise this would've happened at some point in the future. You would've left me anyway, I know that. When he comes back, you'll have to go to him – I know that too. Only... don't bring him here to do your bonking, I couldn't handle that.'

I cringe at his baseness. 'Of course not. It's not like that anyway, but you wouldn't understand.'

Mal couldn't look any worse if I'd punched him. He takes a sip of his tea and with a brave half-smile, 'Well, if it doesn't work out with him, I'll even help you to get set up in a flat. How's that?'

Why is he being so nice?

Grace avoids me. Gets ready for school and runs out the front door.

The phone rings. I take a deep breath and pick it up.

It's Pauline. 'I've just heard about your problems – get yourself over here cause Ron's phoning you at nine, OK?'

'I'll be there right away!'

I welcome the relief of being out on the open road. My spirit can breathe again. As I drive, the sun lights the wild flowers at the edge of the lanes, the green fields stretch to the horizon. When I arrive, Pauline's been doing some much-needed spring-cleaning. All her sofas and chairs are out on the front grass. The door is open. I walk in, but she suggests we sit on the sofas outside in the sun.

'Now,' says Pauline, lighting a cigarette and looking intently at me with her brown eagle eyes. 'What's been happening at home?'

I offload the events of the past two days and watch her expression. I can't read anything into it but it helps to know she's been talking to Ron. Dead on nine her phone rings. I jump up and answer it.

'Julie?'

'Yeah, it's me.'

'Oh, God, I've been so worried, in fact, I've been so worried I got stuck into the vino and told Claudette everything. So she's none too happy now, either. She thinks you're going to hurt me and you're just using me for the final... end!'

'Oh? But you know that's not true, don't you?'

He heaves a big sigh. I can hear the impatience in his voice. 'Yeah. We can go ahead now, then? Now everything's worked out?'

Everything?

There's a pause. I can't believe he's being so calm about this.

'If Mal had harmed you, I would've got someone to go round and fix him – I would've found a way.'

Oh God. I never envisaged violence.

'Well, thankfully, it hasn't come to that.'

'Oh, mate! You'll never know how worried I've been. I just walked around the house all day.'

'Me too. It's so good to hear your voice. I miss you.'

'Yeah, me too. Look, I won't be able to phone much now – I've gotta save to come back, but I'll write. And I'll send you a cassette with my voice on it so you can play it in the car. I'll send it to Shirley's, OK? I love you.'

'I love you too. I wish you were here.'

'Yeah, me too. But right now I gotta go. Try not to worry. Speak soon. Bye.'

Cold desolation grips me. I sit with Pauline, we talk for another hour, but despite the sunshine I feel cold inside and ill.

I leave Pauline's and drive to Shirley's. Her door is open so I walk in. She comes to see who it is, her two children in tow. She tells them to watch *Neighbours* while I tell her what's happened.

'Oh, no, Julie,' she breathes. 'Are you all right?'

'I think so. Just feel so... lost.'

'I can imagine.'

Her motherly instinct takes over and she makes me a cup of coffee and a sandwich. I stay with her into the afternoon. The more I talk, the better I feel.

But when I finally go home my heart sinks – Mal's car is on the drive. He's wallowing in self-pity, walking about the living room as if he's destined for the gallows. He hasn't been to work all day and for some unknown reason, this makes me angry.

He looks at me with a desperate expression. 'What am I going to do without you? I don't know what to do. Tell me what to do,' he whimpers.

He's obviously been crying. I never realised how much this break-up would hurt him – never thought he loved me that much. But it's too late, I feel coldly detached, like it's happening to someone else. 'Look. I think you need to go and talk to someone – someone who's been there, someone who understands. Why don't you go over to Jim and Jean's? Give them a ring?'

'I don't know. I'm not like you – I haven't got any friends.'

'Yes you have. You can talk to Jim, can't you?'

'I suppose so.'

I go upstairs to get away from his cloying self-pity. The phone rings. I run down to answer it before Mal picks it up. It's Grace. She's staying round Claire's for tea. I heave a sigh of relief and go back upstairs. I hear Mal lift the phone. I'm pleased he's seen reason. Jean and Jim are our mutual friends who live in the same village. Jim works with Mal at head office. Jean is older than me and we sometimes go shopping together. They met on holiday one year and have both been through a divorce. Hopefully they'll have some advice for Mal.

I hear him open the front door – I can breathe again – the house to myself. I crave Ron's strength but the black cloud of guilt is my only companion. I open a bottle of Corbières, take a few gulps and think about something to eat. But I can't face food; instead I knock back two more glasses of red wine.

Mal comes back at nine and tells me Jean gave him dinner. I'm thankful for her concern but wonder if she'll sympathise with me when she sees me. Mal seems a bit better after talking to them, but they only gave him practical financial advice.

'I'll agree to a two year separation with a view to an automatic divorce. The only thing I don't want is for you to take Grace away from me – you're not having her as well.'

This is a surprise. I haven't even thought that far ahead.

'No, of course not. I'll never do that.' But I can't tell him whatever it takes, I just want to be released.

THURSDAY 23 APRIL 1987

I go to do Pauline's hair.

Ron rings. 'How are you?'

'I'm fine. Everything's fine. How about you?'

'Claudette's being awkward over it now and again, but that's how it is. I'm glad you're OK. You sound happier.'

'That's cause I'm talking to you!'

'Ha, yeah, I know what you mean. Oh, mate, it won't be long before we hold each other again. I'm even more determined to get back sooner now everything's worked out. I'll write to you at the weekend and tell you my plans. But I must go now. I don't know how much I'm racking up on this phone bill. Catch you later.'

I reluctantly put the down phone. I begin to cut Pauline's hair – she fancies a new style but my mind's not on it.

'You can come round any time for a chat, you know.'

'Thanks Pauline.'

She forgets I'm cutting her hair and turns her head to look at me. The scissors slip and blood spurts from my finger. 'Damn!'

'What is it?'

'Cut myself.'

She runs to fetch a plaster but it's not the wound that brings tears to my eyes.

MONDAY 27 APRIL 1987

The weekend passed uneventfully. I'm grateful for the respite but it's short-lived.

This evening, Mal has a last ditch attempt at saving our marriage. While Grace is in bed, he tries to appeal to my conscience as a mother.

'You can't walk out on Grace while she still needs you. She's at a crucial stage in her life with exams coming up.' He looks down at his hands. 'You've got to be with her; she's turning into a young lady; she needs her mum. She needs you... and so do I. Oh, Ju, can't we give it another try?'

It's a plea from the heart but I have to be completely truthful with him however much it hurts. There's no easy way to tell him.

'It would never work... I don't love you.'

He looks at me as if I've run him through with a knife. I can see no way out – if I leave, I won't be able to live with myself. If I stay, I will end up hating Mal. I'm emotionally trapped.

Will Ron wait for me for as long as it takes? If the answer is no, I will have lost him a second time and I can't bear it.

TUESDAY 28 APRIL 1987

Mal's gone to work. Grace is in her bedroom getting ready for school. I knock on her door.

'Can I come in?'

She nods, her back to me.

'I've decided I'm not going. Yet.'

Have I just signed my life away?

She puts some books in her rucksack, still with her back to me. 'You could stay till I finish school.'

Has Mal been talking to her?

'OK. This is very difficult for me, you know?'

She nods again. It's difficult for both of us.

It's obvious she doesn't want to talk so I go back downstairs, do some washing up and pack my hairdressing box for the day.

I watch Grace walk down the road, and close the door. Pauline rings to tell me Ron phoned this morning to say he's going to ring there tomorrow at nine. She's had a long chat with him and he's got his flight booked already! I'll be without a car tomorrow – it's going in for a service – so I ask her to phone me at home.

Trying to keep body and soul together, I do my customers and come in at lunchtime.

Mal rings. 'I'm going to make it easy for you.'

'Huh, no one can make it easy for me.'

'I can't hold you against your will – you're like a caged bird.'

'Don't you understand? It's my feelings I'm battling with – I've still got to live with the guilt.'

'What do you want to do?'

' I don't know. I don't know anything anymore.'

'OK. I'll talk to you tonight.'

I go about my work in a dream. I can't remember whose hair I've done or where I've been.

I'm going mad.

When Mal comes home in the evening, he wants an answer. I look him straight in the eye. 'You know what I'm going to say, don't you?'

'Yeah. You're going. You've made your mind up. There's no going back, I know that.'

I feel a wave of relief but I know this won't be the end.

WEDNESDAY 29 APRIL 1987

I'm alone when Ron phones to tell me he's coming home on Sunday 24 May.

'My plane arrives thirteen thirty-five at Heathrow.'

'I'll be there.'

I can hear the smile in is his voice. 'I'll give you the biggest kiss and cuddle you've ever had at Heathrow. God! I've been going through hell at home, just like you. But it's all gonna be worth it for both of us. Just wait and see. I can't wait to see you again.'

I picture myself counting off the days. 'I love you. I always have and I always will.'

'I always will, now. That diary's made me realise a lot of things. I've had my fun... now I want to settle down.'

'Your fun's just beginning!'

We laugh together, the first time for ages.

'I've got the photos back of that day in the country. They're great. Happy smiling faces. Oh, you're so easy to be with!'

'I feel the same. It's wonderful, isn't it?'

'Yeah, it is. There's a lot to look forward to. Listen, I know it's bank holiday there, I'll phone you at Pauline's on Tuesday, OK?'

'Of course. I'll be there.'

SPRING BANK HOLIDAY MONDAY

I come home at 4 o'clock after spending the weekend at Mum's. But I can cut the atmosphere with a knife. This is Steve's doing. Steve and his daughters, Nicola and Debbie, stayed the weekend and left this morning. Mal and Steve have been comparing notes – they're in the same situation – Rose, Steve's wife, filed for divorce only a few weeks ago but her situation seems run-of-the-mill compared to mine.

I cook dinner. We eat in silence. I can't stand this much longer. I open a bottle of Côte du Rhone and down three glasses. I open another and share it with Mal. He says he wants to talk soon about the finances – he's frightened he's going to lose the lot – it's going round and round in his head. This makes me angry. It isn't about the money.

'Look, I'm the one that'll lose everything, as you put it. The money doesn't matter to me – I don't want half the house or anything else. I just wanna be free!'

My point-blank honesty shocks him but I have to make him see how important this is.

TUESDAY 5 MAY 1987

At Pauline's, Ron rings true to his word. I can feel his urgency coming down the line. 'When you pick me up from the airport, we can go straight to Petersfield for a couple of days, make some plans.'

'I've already thought of that. Mal and Grace will be in Menorca for a whole week. We booked it ages ago. They go on the Saturday.'

'That's great. I'm phoning from a call box – it's difficult at home. I've been to hell and back, like you. Claudette's being very awkward. Anyhow, I've sold virtually everything now. I'm not penniless, but by the time I've paid for my plane ticket there won't be much left.'

'Oh dear.' I feel bad for him but I also want to tell him how bad *I* feel. I need some support. 'I'm living on my nerves at the moment. Mal's being very difficult.'

'Yeah, you're going through the same as me. But I love you. It'll all be worth it...'

The pips sound. I hang up.

Twenty minutes later he rings back. 'Like the words of the Stevie Wonder song, I just called to say I love you! I know what you're going through – just grin and bear it. It won't be long till we hold each other again.'

'I love you too. I wish you were here. Now.'

'I know. Just remember what I said. It won't be long. Catch you later.'

I know Ron's trying to lift my spirits but as soon as I put the phone down I feel desolate.

In the evening, Mal tells me he's going down to see his parents tomorrow to tell them what's going on. He's not looking forward to it.

'No changing your mind? If I go down there tomorrow, that's it. No turning back.'

I nod. 'Yes, I know.'

'You're sure?'

Why does he keep asking me?

'Yes. I'm sure', I blurt out.

However, the dark seeds of doubt have been sown yet again.

WEDNESDAY 6 MAY 1987

Mal didn't get much sleep last night for thinking about what he's got to do today. Nor did I. How will I ever be able to live with myself? Grace looks so miserable this morning. It's a dream I'm not allowed to have. It's driving me mad.

I speak to Grace again before she goes to school and again she makes me feel really bad about leaving. The chance for a new life is slowly slipping away. I'm torn, torn between my duty towards Mal and Grace, and my love for Ron and a new life.

I can't stand this. I'm going under.

I ring Mal at work. 'Don't go down your mum's tonight...I can't go through with it!'

'I'm coming home!'

I pace the living room floor and think about the next step. I take a deep breath and ring Ron in Australia, hoping he'll understand. 'I'm sorry, I can't go through with it ...my conscience won't let me...I think I'm going mad.'

His anger pours down the phone. 'Do you know what you've just done? I've sold everything I've ever worked for in fourteen years!'

A long uncomfortable pause, then a deep sigh. He's thinking, makes clicking noises with his tongue. As if he's won a battle with himself he says, 'OK, I've still gotta come back to England...I'll lose a lot of money if I cancel my plane ticket. Look, don't commit yourself to Mal yet...I won't phone anymore till I come back... let you get your head together.' He blows out another long sigh. 'We've got a lot going for us. You're a long time dead – remember that,' he shouts. 'Think about it!'

I put down the phone and collapse into sobs. I'm frightened Ron thinks less of me now, yet I can't put Mal and Grace through such misery. I feel at the hub of it all. Forces outside my control have picked me up and thrown me into a whirlpool of hideous chaos. I hate myself but I'm powerless to act.

Mal comes home, takes one look at me and knows his hopes are dashed. In an attempt to soothe us both he takes me to a pub in Shepreth for lunch. I can't believe he feels sympathy for me after all the pain I've put him through. I don't deserve it.

Why is he being so nice? So caring?

But I don't want to be with him. I feel a fraud. I can't eat. I don't know what's on my plate. I keep having terrifying whooshes of panic that leave me breathless, heart palpitating.

We get back in the car and his face is creased with worry. He picks up my hand and holds it but I can't look at him – I'm reminded of Ron doing the same in Ashwell. I withdraw my hand. He turns his head away and drives us home.

Grace comes in from school but I can't tell her I'm staying. I ignore her and run upstairs to my sanctuary and sob.

Mal bursts in. 'Look, you can't keep torturing yourself like this. You're never going to share my bed, are you?'

I feebly shake my head.

'I can't have you living like a caged animal. I understand you're in love with the bloke…when he comes back, go to him. Grace and I will have to manage without you.'

I sag with immense relief. I hear Mal say I need to let Grace know what's going on, that it's not nice for her living in this environment. I know this already – he doesn't have to tell me.

Trying not to look happy, I go and tell Grace I've tried to come to terms with staying, but I just can't. She's surprisingly philosophic – it turns out she's been talking to Claire's mum. She told Grace it was no good if I was unhappy. She would have to let me go. Another person on my side. I feel free. At last.

Mal tells me to phone Ron back and stop him worrying. In all this turmoil Mal can still empathise with the man who's caused his misery. I imagine if the two of them ever met they would get on like two brothers separated at birth. But I push the similarities out of my mind. Ron *is* different.

I ring Australia. Ron sounds changed towards me – he puts Claudette on the phone. I wasn't expecting this – I haven't given her a lot of thought up till now, haven't taken her feelings into account at all. I have never asked Ron how she feels. I have assumed there is no love between them but she blows that idea into the ether with her grievances. I feel detached and inadequate in consoling her, it's not my place. She makes it plain that she hates me for what I've done to Ron today. 'Ron's very upset,' she cries in her broad Australian accent. She lays into me, makes it known how well he's thought of and what he's giving up for me. I'm so shocked I'm unable to come back with what I'm giving up. I feel well and truly castigated for causing so much unnecessary worry but feel it was out of my hands.

THURSDAY 7 MAY 1987

Mal goes to see his parents this evening and tells them everything. He's exhausted when he returns but says there was no nastiness, their first concern was for Grace. Another hurdle over.

FRIDAY 8 MAY 1987

Ron rings at Pauline's. He sounds detached, different towards me. 'How are you?'

'I'm fine, thanks. What about you?'

'Yeah, I'm OK now. Claudette's better – I took her out for a meal last night to try and smooth things over. She's accepted it. Things will still be a bit tense but at least it won't be as bad.'

I'm jealous of their friendship. I would like to know how he really feels about her but can't bring myself to ask him.

'Thank heavens for that. Mal's gone to see a solicitor this morning to get some advice. I've said I don't want anything from him, so I will be walking out with nothing – I can't do that to him – he's been through enough.'

There's a slight pause while he thinks about this.

What was he expecting?

'Yeah. That's only fair.'

I don't think he's too happy about this. It's going to be difficult, what with Ron selling all his possessions and me with only the money in my business account.

'I've been to find out about emigration to Australia for you in a couple of years. You have to go for an interview and a medical and I would have to sponsor you.'

'Oh, that sounds possible, then.' I haven't given this any thought. I assumed we would be settling in this country; he wanted to come back to England, didn't he?

'I know someone who's opening a new hairdressing salon in Canberra; what d'you think?'

'Yeah, why not?'

I hear him exhale. 'I won't phone anymore now till next Friday but I'm definitely sending you a letter. I still think we've got a battle ahead of us.'

'Yeah, but I think we can cope with anything now.'

He doesn't confirm this. His mind seems elsewhere. 'Still going down to Petersfield from the airport?'

'Of course.'

'We've got a lot of talking to do.'

'We certainly have. Love you.'

'You too,' is all I get back.

Mal comes home in the evening and tells me he's been to see the solicitor. 'If you don't contest the writ it'll all go through in four months. They'll be writing to you. The longer it takes, the more it costs.'

'Of course.'

A gulf of silence. I wonder if he thinks I'll change my mind in view of the circumstances, but I've done all of that – my mind's made up.

He looks at me cagily. 'I read your diary.'

I'm not shocked – I had asked him to read it on Wednesday but he was too upset.

He nods. 'At least now I know how you feel – I can't compete with that.'

TUESDAY 12 MAY 1987

Ron rings at nine.

'I couldn't go till Friday without talking to you. I need some reassurance. I nearly cracked up yesterday... I had a really bad day. I went through what you went through last Wednesday. You still going to spend some time with me when I come back?'

'Of course I am!'

'Good. Claudette's OK now, well, better, but there's still that underlying tension.'

'Yeah, I know what you mean – it's the same for both of us. I'll be sticking to you like glue when you come back!'

'We'll be sticking to each other, cause we've only got each other, now. We've both effectively burned our bridges.'

It's a scary thought but he of all people should realize there is always something you can do, somewhere to go. I try and sound positive. 'Everything will work out. I know it.'

'Yeah, OK. Gotta try and keep the bills down. My phone bill will be about four hundred dollars! Speak to you Friday at Pauline's.'

So the seeds of doubt have been sown there, too. I hope Ron doesn't change his mind now. Where would that leave me?

FRIDAY 15 MAY 1987

8.30am Ron rings me at home. He nearly got an earlier flight – he wants to be back sooner!

'Claudette wants to see me off at the airport – it'll be a bit traumatic for her.'

'Yes, I suppose so. When you rang I had a horrible feeling you were going to tell me something I didn't want to hear.'

'Oh, no. Nothing's gonna stop me now. When you meet me at Heathrow, it's flight QF9 by the way, it'll be just the two of us taking a slow drive down to Petersfield.'

'Lovely. Can't wait!'

'Is everything OK at home?'

'Yeah, everything's fine.'

'Is Mal a bit worried about the move you're making?'

'I think so.'

'Don't worry – we'll work it out.'

I'm feeling more uncertain by the day but I can't tell him. Like he says, we're in it together.

'You've got a letter in the post! I sent it to Shirley's. When I'd sealed it up, I thought of a lot more I could say.'

'I'm looking forward to that. I'll phone you next time – Tuesday.'

'I might be in Canberra. I'll see, I might ring you before.'

'But you've gotta keep the bills down!'

'Oh, who cares!'

MONDAY 18 MAY 1987

Shirley rings at 4pm. Mal's come home early so I have to be careful. I can't allow myself to sound excited.

'You've got a letter here, Julie!'

'OK. I'm coming round.'

I put the phone down and jump into my car.

Shirley gives me the airmail letter with a big smile on her face. 'I'll leave you to read it on your own, Julie.'

With delicious anticipation I peel it open. The pale blue airmail paper is folded and written on on every surface as though he hasn't enough room to fit everything in:

THE PRESENT

Hi mate,

This is the overdue letter I promised you. Well, not long now. I'm glad I phoned you last night (Tuesday 9am your time). Talking to you took a lot of pressure off me. The last few days have really taken their toll on me and I imagine the pressure that you must be under. Not easy is it?

Well, I'll soon be back in the old dart and a brand new start to life with you. It is certainly a future to look forward to and cherish. (Please excuse the writing, I am writing this letter just before I am due to leave for work, so it is rather hurriedly written.)

The time remaining here will be very tense especially as departure time gets closer. Claudette is handling it very well at this time but there are still 11 days to endure.

THE FUTURE

It's really up to us now. We have both effectively burned our bridges, so we really only got ourselves to

113

stand by and support. Christ! What a formidable pair! Watch out world, it's the Julie and Ron drive for prosperity and successful future so don't stand in our way or we will go right over you and leave you stupefied!

I love you dearly, Julie, and I promise to make life for you as happy and prosperous as I possibly can. It will possibly be hard to start with but if we strive together we can achieve anything we set our hearts on. That's what life is all about. The future is now ours; let's go for it. Remember: He who dares, wins.

I LOVE YOU WITH ALL MY HEART
Ron xxxxx etc. phew!!

Gosh. I've never received a letter like it. I read it again, and again, studying his writing, dashed off with such fervour it surprises me. On the one hand it's a bit scary, but on the other, it gives me hope and encouragement.

I find Shirley in her kitchen. There's a big smile on my face.

'I take it it's good news then, Julie?'

I nod. 'Here, you can read it if you like?'

'Oh, I don't feel I ought to, it's too personal.'

'No, go on.' I thrust it into her hand and watch her expression. I need her to know the extent of Ron's love and devotion. It's obvious she thinks it's wonderful.

'Well, Julie. What can I say?'

We talk and laugh together. It's the happiest I've felt for a long time. I drive home and leave the letter in my car.

When I open the front door Mal's face is like thunder.

'You're taking me for a fucking prat – there was another wrong number this afternoon!'

'But that's impossible.'

'Is it?' he shouts. 'Is that where you were just now?'

'No, nothing like that,' I lie.

'I know he rang this morning – still the deceit goes on! He can't fucking wait, can he?'

I've never seen him so angry and I'm worried – Mal's never been a violent man but he might turn nasty now. We give each other a wide birth until he takes Grace down to his parents for half term. As he opens the front door, he turns to me. 'I'm sorry for what I said earlier. Just give me the benefit of the doubt, OK?'

I'm on my own this evening. I have to share Ron's wonderful letter with someone so I decide to ring my old pal Lorn. I haven't spoken to her for months. She's divorced and now lives in Eastbourne. She's had a tough life: her son, Carle, was diagnosed with leukaemia at the tender age of three (but later gained a full remission, thank God), the man she divorced her husband for turned out to be a liar and a cheat and ran off with the barmaid and the takings from their pub. And on top of all that she has OCD (obsessive compulsive disorder). She's now living with a younger man who's come from a well-to-do family but he's into drugs. They are living from hand to mouth, but through all her hardship she retains her sense of humour.

She came to stay with us last October, half term. I remember what she said about Mal: "What's wrong with him, Blue? He's so BORING!" So it wasn't just me. Her face lit up when I told her I intended to send a fortieth birthday card to my boyfriend from twenty years ago. We discussed it one evening on our own, in the red and white box room where I now sleep. She'd asked if I'd been to bed with Ron back in 1966. When I told her I hadn't, she gave me a sideways look.

She had always been into fortune telling and astrology. She did a Rune reading for me and wrote it at the back of my present diary – if only I had heeded the advice my life might not be in such a mess. *'To be forewarned is to be forearmed'*.

'Hello, darlin'!' she says, in her gravelly voice. 'What a nice surprise. How are you?'

I proceed to bring her up to date with all my news while I listen to her gasps and sighs. I can hear the smile in her voice. 'Oh, I'm so pleased for you, Blue, this is what you need! Good for you, go for it.'

I read Ron's latest letter to her.

'That's lovely, I don't know what to say, it's fantastic! Listen, I know this sounds selfish but you've got to think of you now. Grace has got her own life and so's Mal. Keep me in touch and let me know how things work out.'

Tonight, in the red and white box room which has become my sanctuary, I put Ron's letter under my pillow. Time, which was always my enemy with wings, now can't go fast enough.

WEDNESDAY 20 MAY 1987

When I'm on my own, I ring Ron and thank him for his letter.

'The things you write when you're under pressure!' he jokes, making light of it.

But why should he feel the need to apologise? Hadn't he meant all those things?

'I'm still catching the same plane; I'll be at Heathrow at one-thirty on Sunday. Not long now. What you've gotta do is avoid arguments at home.'

'I know.'

There's a pause and I hear him chew his lip. 'Yeah, I won't look very special after twenty four hours on a jumbo jet!'

This doesn't matter to me. All the same, I sense his apprehension.

'Mal said it was hard for him knowing I'll be with you at the weekend and what we'll be doing.'

'Ha, don't worry; after twenty four hours on a jumbo jet there won't be much happening!'

SATURDAY 23 MAY 1987

Last night, Steve, Nicola and Debbie stayed the night in preparation for leaving for Luton airport today to go to Menorca with Mal and Grace. Grace went to a party at Harston; I thought it was silly of Mal to let her go when they all had to get up so early. At eleven-fifteen, Grace rang and asked Mal to pick her up outside The Kings Arms at midnight. I didn't like the sound of it; we didn't know where she was phoning from. I went with Mal to pick her up but when we arrived she was nowhere to be seen. After fifteen minutes there was still no sign of her and I started to panic. I suggested we go to the house where the party was but she wasn't there either. This was madness. We walked up and down the road looking for her, then Mal rang home from a call box. Steve answered and said she was there! I was so relieved: I'd had visions of her disappearance on the news. I was also very angry with her for behaving so irresponsibly. When we got home, I dragged her out of bed and gave a good telling off and told her not to behave like that while they were on holiday. I knew Mal would blame me for not being with them if anything happened.

This morning at 9o'clock the solicitor's letter drops on the mat. Mal hands it to me and waits for my lip to quiver. But I disappoint him.

Fifteen minutes later, Mal and Grace, Steve, Nicola and Debbie leave for Luton airport to go to Menorca. I look at Grace as she goes through the door. 'Enjoy yourself and don't give your dad a hard time.'

She shrugs and turns her back on me, eager to get away with her friends. I don't know if I'm hurt or relieved.

Mal steps outside, hesitates, then smiles self-consciously as he turns back to me. 'Be happy.'

He gets in the car and they drive away. I breathe in the absence of them and fling my arms out, thanking God for the space. I walk into all the empty rooms, like a cat impregnating its territory. I get on with my own preparations for tomorrow and try to ignore my threatening anxiety.

At one-thirty Mal rings from the airport to tell me their flight is delayed; there's a French air traffic controller's strike.

'Are you all right?'

'Yes, I'm fine.'

'Not getting jittery?'

'No. Why should I?'

'Right, then. See you when we get back.'

'Sure.'

He makes me realise how nervous I really am and I wonder if this strike will have any impact on Ron's flight. I keep myself busy, packing, doing odd jobs. I can feel Ron's spirit – I picture him on the plane full of passengers. I keep rehearsing my journey to Heathrow and planning what to wear and what to take, counting down the hours.

SUNDAY 24 MAY 1987

At six-fifteen I wake with a jolt and my heart thuds against my ribs like a big machine coming to life. My stomach churns. This is it, the big day. I keep telling myself to keep calm and everything will be all right.

I get up and check the road map to memorise the journey, again. I mustn't take a wrong turn. I must look cool, calm and collected when I greet Ron at the airport. He won't appreciate me looking like a frightened rabbit.

I make a cup of tea. The phone rings. It's Steve – he wants a phone number. He sounds panicky.

'Is everything all right out there?' I ask.

'Yeah, everything's fine. It's just me. Trouble with Rose,' he sighs. 'Listen, I'm sorry to bother you. It's OK. Forget it.'

This doesn't do anything for my nerves.

At eight-fifteen the phone rings again. This time it's Jean. 'I just thought I'd ring, see how you are.'

'I'm fine,' or I would be without all these phone calls.

'Now, keep calm, Julie; this is the big one! Give yourself plenty of time to get there, get a coffee and settle down. What time does his plane come in?'

'One-thirty. I'll leave about ten-forty-five.'

'Good girl. Now, don't panic. It's all going to happen. You must be really excited?'

'Yeah.'

'OK. I'll let you get on. If you need anything, you know where I am.'

'Thanks, Jean.'

I put the phone down, wipe my palms. My heart is thumping. I breathe in and out slowly.

I'm surprised Jean rang – she's batting for both sides, then?

I go to the kitchen and pour out some breakfast cereal and milk, but every mouthful is like sawdust.

I have a shower. The warm water cleanses and soothes my aura, making me feel revitalised. I take particular care blow-drying my hair, making sure it looks just right. I remember Ron's preference for long hair and try to pull it to its full length.

Ten forty-five. I take a last glance in the mirror – my Prince of Wales check suit with a peplum and a white lace high-necked blouse, black patent shoes.

I pick up my case.

Well, this is it.

I breathe in the fresh air and close the front door behind me.

It's a good journey; I've rehearsed it so well in my mind it couldn't be anything else.

At ten past twelve I arrive at Heathrow, park in the multi-storey and make my way to the arrivals lounge at Terminal 4. It's buzzing with people. I go to the loo then take Jean's advice – buy a cup of coffee and a sandwich. I find a vacant table. The coffee is boiling hot. I will it to cool down. I feel self-conscious – a woman on her own in this massive cafe. I keep looking at my watch and start to imagine us greeting each other with huge hugs and kisses.

I check the screen for the arrival of flight QF9 from Sydney. Yes! There it is: estimated arrival time 13.50. ON TIME.

Not long now.

I wait. And wait. It seems like forever. I keep seeing people go off to meet their friends and relations, loved ones. I go to the loo again and come back to check the screen.

FLIGHT QF9 LANDED!

Oh God!

I hurriedly make my way to the barrier. There are streams of people with trolleys filtering through from the plane, being met with hugs and kisses.

Suddenly, he's there. I see him before he sees me. He looks tired and flustered, the huge trolley is piled high with his suitcases and other belongings. He grabs one of the bags before it falls on the floor. He looks along the rows of people then his eyes meet mine, a tiny glimmer of recognition. I go over and kiss him on the cheek but there is no response – he's too intent on getting out of the airport.

'Where's your car parked?' his first words to me.

I tell him what level it is. He bundles his trolley into the lift and we go up in silence. We are still silent as he walks his trolley to my car. He looks agitated as he puts his entire luggage in the boot, slams it.

He sits heavily and bangs the door. 'Twenty four hours I've been travelling. I'm absolutely shattered.'

This wasn't what I had in mind.

"Jeez', I kept thinking, 'She'd better show up after all this!"

I start the car and drive out of the car park and try to focus on the road.

He hasn't kissed me or said I look nice.

Ron directs me to his sister Sally's and I'm relieved that he takes control. He starts to relax a little on the journey but there is no conversation. I feel like a taxi driver.

We finally arrive outside a very smart, newly built house on a small estate. The front door opens and out comes a woman with light brown hair and a neat skirt and top. She's smiling broadly. Ron quickly gets out the car and rushes to greet her.

I follow but stand back.

Ron's all smiles. 'Sal! This is Julie.'

She doesn't look any different to the last time I saw her in 1966.

'Oh, I remember Julie!' she says holding out her arms. She gives me a hug and I feel relieved, comforted. 'Come on in.' She turns to Ron. 'I bet you're exhausted?'

He nods and mutters something about the journey.

We follow Sally into her bright and airy lounge. My eyes dart around surreptitiously; Sally has good taste. The lounge is decorated in pastel colours with Indian rugs scattered on the wood floor.

There's an air of expectancy as Sally bustles about pandering to her brother's needs. 'Make yourself at home, Julie. I know what Ron wants – a nice hot shower!'

'Yeah, you bet!' He turns to me, 'My sister Sal knows me well!'

Ron goes off to the bathroom while Sally makes me a cup of tea. I perch on the edge of one of her squishy sofas and hope Ron doesn't take too long.

Sally comes back breezily with the tea and biscuits on a tray. She's eager to hear all the events leading up to today but I feel guilty for what I've left behind and don't want her to pass judgement. 'How are you, Julie?'

'Oh, OK.'

'It's been a bit of a bumpy ride, hasn't it?'

I nod. *You're not kidding.*

'I can't imagine what you've been through. But everything should be all right now Ron's home.'

I nod again and feel exactly the same as I did in 1966.

'It must've been traumatic for your husband and daughter?'

'Yes.' I take a sip of tea and hope she changes the subject. I don't want to revisit it all; I want to put it behind me.

The rest of her family come in noisily and drop their muddy boots in the hall. Sally asks how the football match went. It turns out they won two-nil. They all come in to meet me. Unlike Sally, Martin has changed a lot – his hair is almost white and he's put on weight. Their two sons, Richard and Christopher both primary school age, are all smiles as if I'm a long-lost relative being welcomed back into the fold. They all seem extremely grateful for what my fortieth birthday card has set in motion. The scene is set for a happy homecoming and I begin to relax.

Ron comes back looking refreshed and larger than life, wearing a white hooded sweatshirt with AUSTRALIA printed across the front. It attracts attention, the exact reaction he wants, of course. Sally comes in with two plates of chicken salad and a bottle of chilled white wine. The table is set for two; our first meal together to celebrate Ron's decision to come back to England. We chink glasses but the food takes its time to slip down. I'm very apprehensive about our first night together; nothing has been mentioned.

Ron, on the other hand, eats his salad and drinks his wine like a condemned man. He picks up his glass of wine and takes a gulp. 'Mm, that's nice!' Examines the bottle. Caught up in the excitement of being the focus of attention, he seems unaware of my feelings. The family place me in the limelight as the reason for Ron's homecoming and make me feel as if I'm the answer to all their dreams. If this is anything to go by, our life together should be amazing, but I can't help feeling anxious.

The family are watching television. Ron squats down beside my chair and gazes lovingly into my eyes. The look speaks volumes. Love fills every fibre of my being and everything else in the room disappears. I know he feels the same.

After we've rested Ron directs me as we drive to Lottie and Jack's and park my car outside a semi on a new estate – this is where we are expected to stay, Sally owns the house and rents it out but there are no occupants at present. I was unaware of these arrangements until now. We walk to Lottie and Jack's nice little bungalow along the road. Here we have another lovely welcome. Lottie and Jack don't look much different from what I remember – she still has the same hairstyle and he still has the same horn-rimmed glasses and the same amount of baldness. It's as if time has stood still for them.

Lottie greets me. 'Hello, love. How are you? It's been a bit traumatic these last few weeks, hasn't it?'

I nod and smile, so does Ron.

'Still, never mind. Hopefully everything will be all right now,' she says, more to herself than to us.

We stay for a chat, Jack still making the jokes and Lottie taking the conversation seriously. Nothing has changed for them.

'The house is all ready, love.' Lottie tells Ron. 'I expect you'll want to get off now, and relax.'

We walk back along the road to the semi where I parked the Nova. Ron shows me around like an estate agent. It's nicely furnished in muted shades, although on a budget. No point in buying expensive furnishings for a rented house.

'Well, this is home for as long as we need it! What d'you think?' says Ron, eagerly watching for my reaction.

'Very nice.'

'I think Sally and Martin have done a good job of decorating this place.'

We unload the car and take our luggage up to the spare room. I notice this single bed is unmade, while the double in the main bedroom is all ready and waiting.

Oh, God.

Ron reads my thoughts. 'Everyone will be thinking we've had sex but I don't want it to be like that; it's not about *that*. I'm sure, that when they knew I'd met you in London, they thought we'd taken a room, but it wasn't like that. Nothing sordid. This is something special and I wasn't going to sully it.'

He's thinking along the same lines as me, then.

But I still can't believe this is happening. It's unreal, as if I'm watching it all from a distance.

We sit in the living room while he tells me about the audiotape he's recorded but never got round to sending. He puts it on and leaves me to listen to it on my own. It explains a lot about how he was feeling at the time when Mal had found out about us at Easter.

"Hi Julie, it's me, Ron. Nice to get the opportunity to talk to you again and not have to worry about who's listening in. Oh, God, when you broke the news to me about Mal finding out about us, when he went off his brain, you wouldn't believe how I was feeling. I was so scared for you. In fact, I broke down in front of Claudette, so she got upset and now we've all gone through the same...bloody fight. But the thing with Claudette and I is that... things have been getting bad for some time and it's just gotta come to an end. Mal and Grace've got the rest of their lives to live, so has she, so have us.

(Deep sigh) "Geez I'm looking forward to getting back and seeing you again. It's nice talking to you on the phone but unfortunately, phones are very limited, just a cold piece of plastic. It's not... not the same as being there with you, hugging you. It's now one week and two days since I last saw you, and held you.

"Andrew's been talking today of his plans for expanding the business, blah, blah. But I'm not...I'm not sure when to tell him about my plans to leave Australia. I might...I don't know...there's still money coming in, I've got a large estate car I'm driving around in so I might delay telling him. I've got a lot of things to sell – got records to sell, the boat, a dinghy, an outboard motor...but you know all of this. Got a lot of stuff in the garage to sort out, so the estate car will come in very handy.... Fourteen years of hoarding! See what you're doing to me?... you can straighten me out that way!

"Oh, our future, mate! Doesn't it look bright, and beautiful? Get back... meet you in London... I think we're still gonna have to be a bit tactful on that, cause er... if they know what it's about...and er...

"Hello, I'm getting dried up for things to say!... It's just coming up to six thirty on the Friday night. And I've been humping; large heavy boxes on my own all day. I don't think my muscles have been put through so much strain in their life. I ache. Still, keeps me fit. Maybe even tone up my body a bit! You don't wanna see some fat, flabby thing....not used to fat flabby things! (Chuckle) I won't say any more about that!

"Gee, it's hard to sit in front of a tape recorder and keep rabbiting on. I really want to be with you, and hold you. It's been a long time...twenty years. We've had three short times together... then we were restricted to where we could go and what we could do, always worried that someone's gonna... notice us. Still, we've got plenty of time to make up for, plenty of time. There's country walks to look forward to, dining out, evenings at home. I'm really looking forward to it...really looking forward to it...

"Claudette's still bloody upset. She says she's never gonna love another man in her life. Apparently I'm the second bloke who's broken her heart. When she was twenty two, her boyfriend went over seas, and when he came back, said he's got another girl...ta-ta.

Now she thinks I'm doing the same thing, thirteen years, fourteen years later. I don't know. Maybe it's just her way of making me feel bad. But I'm not gonna change my mind.... definitely not gonna change my mind. I for one have made my pledge. I've set my plans, I've made my decision, my future's ahead of me and you're part of it.

(Pause tape)

"CORRECTION! You're not A part of it; you are THE part of it, the major part. You know, what shitted me off about Claudette's reaction and also Mal's reaction...they knew we'd met in London...thought we'd got up to things, taken a room... but that was further from the truth as you know. But they don't believe us. They can only think of sordid things. But I recognised it for what it was. We have something...precious here. And I wasn't gonna spoilt it, mar it, whatever you wanna say...I wasn't gonna do that...

"Er...I'm sitting here drinking a can of Foster's, which is what we do in Australia, of course... but I'm only gonna have one can, cause I've gotta drive.

"You know, when I told my mates, Darren and Kevin, about you and about my plans to leave Australia, their comments were, 'Well, we couldn't understand why you and Claudette stuck together...' But old habits are hard to break. We do possess a lot here, but happiness is far, far more important. You can always get those things again. You go out, you work hard and you buy those things... if that's what you're into. What I'm into is...I'm over forty now...dare I say it? You're not far off it?! Only eighteen, nineteen when we first met. That's right. The Black Prince, Bexley. And with horror I'm thinking of Auckland Street, Vauxhall! What a bloody place THAT was!... But for the short time we knew each other... yeah, well. Plenty of time to talk about that. Plenty of time.

"But for the time remaining, I'm working hard... come back, put it in the bank, give me something to start with. And hopefully, I'll land myself a very good job... Nice country cottage somewhere? Mmm ..But wherever we end up, there'll always be a lot of old dames, old ladies, wanting their hair done...or ladies who would like a nice cream tea. Twinings or Fortnum and Mason special tea! Julie's tearoom. Mm, got a nice ring to it. Very English. Ha, keep going, Gee, what a dream, but dreams can come true. If you dream hard enough, you start working towards it, it becomes practical, becomes achievable. You'll be able to offer them a blue rinse set at the same time to go down with their cup of cha!!

"Oh, Geez, is that the time? I've gotta get going. Look, what I'll do is, I'll think of something else to put on this tape, but for now I'll sign off. Bye Julie.'

There is a pause on the tape. Then, "Hi, love. Well, it's now Monday eight-fifteen in the morning. It's been very awkward over the weekend; Claudette's been hanging around all this time. Being a very temperamental person, I have to be very careful around her, but I think she's finally accepted the fact that I'm going back.

"Most people I've spoken to about my plans say I'm mad. I don't think I'm mad. In fact I'm looking forward to it. I've got Sunday the twenty-fourth as my deadline. But I think it would be easier, better, if it was Wednesday, your day off. You can meet me in London...Anyway, I'll sort something out.

"Oh! Guess what? My accountant rang me...I've got a tax cheque coming for two thousand dollars, so that helps me as well. I hope to realise three and a half thousand dollars for the boat, five hundred to a thousand for the records and a hundred for the hi-fi. Claudette's umming and arring about that but when she realises what a bargain it is...

"Australia is full of plans for the Bi-Centennial here at the moment. It's gonna be ONE BIG celebration. Two hundred years, the tall ships and the First Fleet sailing through the heads...It'll be really something and hopefully make America's celebrations look silly! I'm thinking we could come back for that...if we're together, and I've every confidence that we will be, we can go together and you can have a look at Australia; see what you think to it.

"Well, the challenge is there, we've made the pledge to each other. We're both giving up a lot, ...you won't have er... too much trouble getting away from Mal but then there's Grace...But no one's gonna stand in my way for my happiness, OR yours. I'll come back and we'll stand side by side and go for it! Who dares wins!

"But for the time remaining, discretion is the best thing at the moment.

"Always thinking of you. (softly) Always thinking of you. Catch you a little later. Bye-bye."

Ron sounds so positive that we're doing the right thing, but my stomach is churning. He's pinned every hope, every dream on me. It's a lot to live up to. He really believes in our future together. 'He who dares wins'. It's all so powerful. I can hear him in and out of the rooms upstairs, sorting out his belongings, putting things away.

He runs downstairs with a video and puts it in the player. 'I've got something you'll be interested in...this is recorded from a breakfast programme in Australia; it's the Moody Blues, remember them?'

I nod, 'Of course.'

He looks at me intently. 'I think you'll find this quite significant.'

I settle down to watch it with him, but nothing could have prepared me for what I was about to see. It's the story of a boy and girl who met in the 1960s, lost touch, and then find each other again in the present day. It's our story! The fashions are exactly the same, the cars, the motor scooters, the hairstyles and I'm back at the Black Prince all those years ago. The track *Your Wildest Dreams* could have been written for Ron and me. It's unbelievable. Goose bumps run over my body, right down to my toes.

Justin Hayward is singing.
'Once upon a time,
Once when you were mine,
I remember skies, reflected in your eyes,
I wonder where you are,
I wonder if you think about me,
Once upon a time in your wildest dreams.'

Ron knows by my expression that it's struck a cord. 'What d'you think?'

I'm speechless for a moment. I shake my head, unable to drag my eyes from the screen. 'It's amazing! I can't believe it.'

'Yeah,' he nods, satisfied. 'thought you'd like it.'

'I love it.' My eyes are fixed to the screen until the very end. 'Can you play it again?'

He rewinds it for me then goes upstairs to unpack some more of his things.

I'm mesmerized. How thoughtful of him and how amazing that it should reflect our story so well!

He comes back downstairs and strides into the room.

'It's really significant, isn't it? But he,' he says, pointing to Justin Hayward, 'loses his woman again. That's not gonna happen to us.'

He kisses me softly and I see the love reflected in his eyes, like the words of the song. They linger on mine. This is our first kiss of the day and I'm thrown into a panic about the forthcoming night.

He produces some more presents: a box of miniature bottles of French perfume and an LP of Andrew Lloyd Webber songs – *Performance*. We've only been together a short time but he knows what I like.

He takes my hand. 'Come on, let's go buy a bottle of champagne. We need to celebrate!'

We walk into town and I welcome the exercise and the fresh air. It gives my stomach something to work on. Spaced out by the day's events, I hang back in the local Spar shop, while he goes in search of the alcohol section. He buys a bottle of Moet et Chandon. I baulk at the price but he doesn't turn a hair.

Then he smiles, 'Hang on, I need a toothbrush. I always make a point of buying a new toothbrush when I go away.'

I follow him to the toiletries but the only one he can find is a child's Tommy Tippee toothbrush.

'You can't use that!'

'Why not? I'm a big kid, after all. It's just that my toys have got bigger and more expensive!'

'What toys?'

'Boats, cars. You name it...'

I am swept along on his euphoria without asking any more questions. We come back to the house and he opens the bottle in the kitchen. BANG! the cork shoots up to the ceiling. He catches the fizzy champagne in a glass, licks his fingers.

He hands it to me. 'Here. Mustn't waste any!'

He pours another for himself and drinks before the bubbles have settled. We chink glasses.

'I love you, Julie. Do you have a middle name?'

'Mm. Ann.'

'I love you, Julie Ann.' He kisses me with all the feeling that's been pent up for weeks. I feel giddy.

'What about you?' I manage. 'Do you have a middle name?'

'Yeah, Edward,' he takes another gulp of champagne.

I try it out to see how it sounds. 'Ronald Edward.'

This makes him smile. I still can't believe this is happening; to have Ron back in my life after twenty years and him declaring his love for me. It's just incredible.

'Let's take the rest to bed with us.'

My alarm bells are ringing; my heart is pounding in my throat.

He stares at me. 'Yeah, although we'll be sharing the same bed, I don't want anything to happen. It's not about **that.**' A cheeky little boy grin. 'Everyone will be thinking we have, but we'll know we haven't!'

We go upstairs and get undressed but although he's stressed nothing sexual will happen, I can't help feeling like a virgin bride on her wedding night. Although I keep my underwear on I feel naked. I never sleep in nightwear, have always preferred to sleep nude since I was married, but I'm frightened my wild abandon would pass on the wrong message. I'm not ready. He pours another two glasses of champagne and gets into bed. I can't remember doing anything like this before and feel stripped of normality. He drains his glass and I'm amazed when he instantly falls into oblivion. I look at the man lying next to me dressed only in his underpants with the boxing Kangaroos printed on them. A smile tugs at my lips; he's quite a character. But I feel it's a force outside our control that has thrown us together. Our love lies suspended at the same stage as it was twenty years ago, as if the spell will be broken if we attempt to make love.

I lay awake most of the night and watch the dawn break.

BANK HOLIDAY MONDAY 1987

5am. Ron opens his eyes dreamily. Puts a warm arm out towards me, wriggles slightly. Kisses me. 'Good morning, Julie Ann.'

'Good morning.'

He waits, then says, 'Ronald Edward.'

'All right. Good morning, Ronald Edward.'

'That's better.'

'That was my dad's middle name, Edward.'

'You miss your dad, don't you?' he says, propping his head up on his arm.

I nod. 'I do. I'll always miss him; it's been ten years but it still seems like yesterday.'

He cuddles me and strokes my hair. We talk about our feelings and what it means to love and lose someone and about things that have happened over the years. One day I will have to go into details about how my dad died but I'm not ready for that. Not yet. My dad was a big part of my life. When he died, part of me died with him.

'I noticed you brought some of your dad's classical records with you.'

'Yeah. I'd like to play them sometime. See what you think. Do you like classical music?'

'Some of it.'

'Ravel's Bolero?'

A light dawns. 'Oh, yeah. I'd forgotten about that!'

An hour later Ron makes tea and we sit in the living room watching the breakfast news. His resumes are spread out on the coffee table in front of him, and I'm in my dressing gown in the armchair. He's intent on organizing his resumes in order to get a good job, hoping twenty years in the music industry won't account for nothing.

The AIDS epidemic has recently exploded onto the news with powerful adverts condemning casual sex, but if you must, always use a condom.

He looks pointedly at me. 'I know you're all right.'

I wait a while, then ask, 'and you?'

He smiles. 'Yeah. Been celibate for three years!'

Is it true? And if it is, what sort of relationship did he have with Claudette?

I drink my second cup of tea, still in my dressing gown. He keeps making tea as if to reinforce his decision to come back to England. Maybe it's the fact that I've had no sleep but I feel horribly exposed, out of my comfort zone. We talk some more. He expects a lot of England. Australia is a positive, go-ahead country by all accounts and he wants England to be the same.

He's brought bundles of photographs with him and lays them out on the dining table; mostly of the outdoors – him on boats in the sunny Sydney harbour. Another indication of what he's left behind.

Does he have any idea how hard it is for me, the enormous guilt I feel at leaving Grace to be with him? I am uncomfortable with all this. My heart is thumping really hard. I hope he can't see it. I don't want him to see me as a shivering wreck.

Another topic on the news is the Cold War. Ron points out that President Ronald Reagan has the power to press the RED button if he wants to and so end the world with a big bang.

'Have you thought where you want to be if that happens?' Ron asks.

I have never given this any thought. Tend to forget it, put it to the back of my mind. But he wants an answer. 'No. But I've thought about who I want to be with.'

I smile at him but he looks away, collects his resumes and goes to put the kettle on, again.

In the afternoon, Ron suggests we go to Harting Fair. He jokes, turning it into a spoonerism. Farting Hair. We giggle like a couple of kids.

I drive, of course, and wonder briefly when he's going to get a car. I park the Nova in a field and we stroll along to where the Morris dancers are performing. This pretty little Hampshire village looks idyllic in the spring sunshine. There are folk bands, clog dancers, and colourful stalls with bunting lining the road. My hand resting in Ron's, I feel my spirit lift as we walk along. He's good to be with. He sees some people he knows and introduces me as 'someone who's come back into my life after twenty years'.

It's real – it's not a dream.

He turns to me when they're out of earshot. 'Vegans – you can always tell. Pasty faces! They always look ill.' Ron's a steak and red wine man. I get the impression most of his mates in Australia are the same.

We mount the steps to The White Hart, a typical country pub, and he orders two lagers – Foster's of course. We sit in the bay window overlooking the street scene. We talk all the time; there's a lot of catching up to do and I'm slowly getting to know this man again. I like what I see and hear: he's very optimistic and positive; makes me realise what I've been missing all these years.

'What about Lofty?' I ask.

'What about him?'

'Well, it's just that you spent so much time together when you were young.'

'Yeah, we did, didn't we? Mm, long time ago. He's happily married with a family, living in Bristol. I think I told you?'

I nod.

'Still the same old Loft; happy-go-lucky.' He looks thoughtful. 'When I met you, you were with a dark-haired girl – can't remember her name.'

'Marie.'

'Yeah, you still in touch?'

I shake my head. 'Lost touch after the accident. She took a job in London. Last I heard she was married to Geoff and living in Ireland.'

'Why Ireland?'

'It's where her parents came from – they were Irish and they went back there to live.'

He nodded. 'I've never been.'

'Me neither.'

'Maybe we'll go one day, surprise her, look her up?'

'I don't have her address.'

'It didn't stop you finding me!'

Caught up in the excitement, Ron drains his glass and orders another while I decline. It's only lunchtime and I'm very conscious of the drink/driving law since Mal lost his licence for twelve months a couple of years ago. If that happened I'd be sunk.

Back at the house, Ron goes to open another can of Foster's but stops himself. He looks at me with a cheeky grin, 'I better not have any more of these – I'm going over the top!' He goes to put the kettle on instead. I have brought some Earl Grey with me; he puts one tea bag in the pot along with a bog-standard one. It seems a good compromise. He smiles. 'One and one. We're learning from each other, aren't we?'

Oh, I do hope so.

I open a packet of Hobnobs and hand him one.

'Mm, they're nice,' he says, finishing the biscuit in two bites. 'Bit too healthy, though!'

We take our tea out to the little garden and sit on the wooden chairs in the sunshine, listening to the birds. We get onto the subject of gardening – he says, 'I like to see a nice garden but don't like doing it. Jim brings his lawnmower round and cuts the grass.'

'Oh? I wouldn't mind doing the garden. I do it anyway...'

He shakes his head. '...You don't have to do that. There'll be enough to do, setting up your business. And another thing – I don't want you working in the evenings. Evenings are for *us* to enjoy,' he says, vehemently.

I can't picture Mal ever saying anything like this! He's always been quite happy for me to work all hours. But Ron does share Mal's love of drink. I quash the niggling similarity.

Ron drains his mug, takes my hand and leads me upstairs. We lie down on the bed together. There's a knot in my belly, wondering if this is finally going to be the moment, but it's like someone's flicked a switch. He's asleep in seconds. I watch him lying there and wonder – how can he just cancel out like that? Maybe it's still the effects of the jet lag. Or is it the alcohol?

But sleep eludes me again. I get up very carefully, trying not to wake him and creep downstairs. I want to collect my thoughts and have some time to myself. But I've only just reached the bottom when he races downstairs as if the house is on fire.

He heaves a sigh of relief and rakes a hand through his hair. 'Oh God, for one horrible moment I thought you'd gone! I thought, "Christ! Where is she? She hasn't left me, has she?" '

I smile. 'No, of course not.'

'I can't lose you now, not after all this.' He pulls me towards him and kisses me long and slow reinforcing his love for me. 'I love you, Julie Ann,' he says, searching my face. 'Say you love *me*.'

'I love you.'

'What's my name?'

'Ron. Ronald Edward,' I say, shyly.

'Say it. Say "I love you Ronald Edward."'

'I love you Ronald Edward.'

'Thank Christ for that!'

This doesn't come easy to me – I've always felt uncomfortable addressing people by name, especially those close to me. Also, I'm not entirely happy that he's so possessive, so different to the person I knew twenty years ago.

'You hungry?' he asks, out of the blue. 'I thought we could go down to the Beefeater.'

'OK.'

I still have no appetite but a good meal might go some way towards quenching my nerves.

We take a stroll downtown to the restaurant. On the way, Ron tells me about his friends in Australia and how they've been behind him on his decision to come back to England.

'I wasn't feeling very positive on my fortieth birthday, I'd had a bad few months and when your card came it was like it came from heaven. All my mates said it was what I needed, things being what they were with Claudette.'

He tells me about his mates taking him out for a meal every night before he came back and pats his stomach. 'Too many! I need to lose a few pounds.'

He weighs fifteen and a half stone. Another similarity he shares with Mal, but I try to ignore it. I know I love him but I'd only been with him for a total of twelve hours before I met him at Heathrow yesterday; there's a large chunk of courtship missing. This coupled with knowing Grace is so upset makes me uncomfortable.

I wonder how they're getting on in Menorca and if they miss me?

We step inside the warm convivial atmosphere of The Beefeater; sounds of cutlery on china and the hum of conversation; delicious aromas. We find a table and each order a steak and chips; Ron orders a bottle of Cotes du Rhone. With the warmth and normality of the restaurant and the help of the rich wine my pulse slows to its usual rhythm.

Our meal arrives and Ron wastes no time in getting stuck in. I realise I'm ravenous and follow suit.

Ron puts his knife and fork down and looks at me. 'For a little woman, you're good on the fang! D'you know what that means?'

I shake my head but I have a pretty good idea.

'It means you can eat! That's good. I like to see that.'

TUESDAY 26 MAY 1987

I get up, have a shower and wash my hair. The warm water running over my body is therapeutic, calms me. I sit on the end of the bed to dry my hair. Ron, still in bed, watches me dry it. I finish and turn to him hoping for a favourable comment. 'What d'you think?'

'Yeah,' he says, 'I'd like to see it a bit longer, but you don't like that, do you?'

A kick in the stomach as I remember that vivid scene from 1967. I put it to one side and search in my make-up bag for my mascara. It's not there. I get up and go to the bathroom. It's not there either. I go back to the bedroom and search again.

'What you looking for?' he asks.

'My mascara.'

'You don't need it. I don't like to see a woman with make-up.'

I don't wear much but I feel naked without it. I begin to wonder what Claudette's like. When he speaks of her on his boat, nipples serving as weather detectors, I picture a dark-haired, sun-kissed woman with no inhibitions who loves the outdoor life.

Nothing like me.

We cook breakfast together – bacon and eggs, toast and tea. Ron's doesn't touch the sides. He sits watching me, waiting for me to finish then mentions his mum's cat. The memory floods in – Boxing Day 1966. The ginger cat. The milk...

'Do you like cats?'

I nod. 'We've got a black one, called Soot,' I start to tell him but it sounds all wrong to be talking about home, but everyone loves Soot – he's a real character. He dips his paw into the remains of our night-time Horlicks and licks it, like Arthur, the cat in the *Whiskas* TV advert.

'I'll get you a cat, a black cat. I like cats.'

I start looking forward to this with mixed feelings. He's going too fast for me. When I don't say any more he changes the subject.

'We're gonna run out of food soon! I thought we could go into Portsmouth and get some shopping?'

I'm happy to go along with this. It'll give me the chance to buy some mascara.

The day is warm and sunny so I wear a thin blouse, skirt and sandals. We jump in the Nova and Ron directs the way.

We go into Petersfield first and stop by Sally's toy shop. She greets us with a big smile, makes us feel like celebrities. She speaks animatedly to Ron about the new stock she's ordered. He's very positive about it and although I can't work up any enthusiasm for toys, I nod and smile, hoping it doesn't show. I excuse myself and pop next door to the chemist. I buy my long-awaited mascara and feel strangely detached from Ron, even vulnerable in this short time. When I return to the toy shop I find Ron leaning on the counter talking in hushed tones with Sally, their heads together. He looks round at me and they stop abruptly.

At Portsmouth I park in the multi-storey. It's tight, but I feel smug when I manage to negotiate the pillars.

'Well done,' he says. 'I hate these places. In Australia the car parks are much more spacious.'

He holds my hand as we walk into town and tells me he has high expectations of this country. My heart starts pounding again. I take deep breaths, trying to steady my nerves.

This is ridiculous. Why do I feel like this?

He stops to look in a camera shop window, intent on selling his photographic equipment for a good price and I wonder how much money he actually has. But I don't feel able to ask him. Everything in the window is a blur, my anxiety gaining on me. He takes me into the *Wimpy* for lunch. He orders the full works – burger, frankfurter, fried egg, tomato, chips and beans, while I settle for a burger. He insists we sit opposite each other.

'You need to see the other person's reaction. It's no good sitting next to them.'

Our meal arrives and he looks at me. 'I'll cook dinner tonight. I don't want you doing all the work; it's important to share everything.'

This sounds wonderful; Mal's quite happy for me to do it all, always has been. It's the way he's been brought up. This new life with Ron will be amazing if I can only stop feeling so nervous.

We finish our meal, get some shopping and walk back to the multi-story. I'm first up the steps and when we reach the top he looks pointedly at me. 'Got a lot of veins on your leg, haven't you?' he says, accusingly.

My heart sinks like a stone. 'The accident,' I mutter.

'That's a shame.'

Does he think I'm damaged goods?

We drive home in silence, his last words ringing in my ears.

We come back and put the shopping away. He shows me the freezer in the garage and goes through what he's planned to cook for the rest of the week. It goes in one ear and out the other.

He pours me a gin and tonic and puts the dinner on. I sit back and enjoy being waited on but conversely I want to show him what I can cook.

We talk about the music I've brought with me. Some of Dad's classical and jazz records amongst the Beatles LPs.

'You brought *The Bolero* to the house once. Remember?'

'Oh, yeah. I did, didn't I? How do you remember so much stuff?'

I answer with a smile and he goes to check on the dinner. When he comes back he looks through his records. 'When was the last time you went to a pop concert?'

I have to think. 'The Beatles in 1963. Lewisham Odeon.' I smile, remembering not being able to hear the music above all the screaming from the excited fans.

Ron shakes his head. 'The Beatles? Christ!' He shakes his head again. 'I'll take you to a concert. You wait. It'll be the best experience you've ever had!'

He goes to the music centre and puts on Bruce Springsteen. I'm not a fan but I listen to it without passing judgement. Then he puts on Simon and Garfunkel whom I can relate to. Says he likes songs with a message, songs with meaning. Like most of their songs, this one is poignant and stirs a memory in me. I listen to the lyrics, remembering that fateful day when my dad died and how much I miss him. I brush the tears away.

Ron notices. 'That's upset you, hasn't it?' he blows out a sigh and puts his drink down. 'I *knew* I shouldn't have put that on! Oh, my poor little love.'

'It's OK, don't worry.'

'No. It's not OK. I should've known better. I won't do that again. I'm so sorry.'

He puts an arm round me, hugs me to him. 'Do you want to talk about it?'

This is Ron's answer to everything no matter how sensitive. I don't know how beneficial this would be right now, but I blow my nose and nod.

Maybe now is the time.

'It's been ten years, but it still seems like yesterday,' I begin. 'It was so awful, the worst day of my life.'

He turns off the music and sits next to me and listens. I have never really addressed the horror of my father's death or the circumstance in which it occurred; I have learned to bury it.

Here goes:

'Dad had fallen on hard times around 1968. Commercial art had taken a dive with the advent of typeset, and Phoenix Studios were feeling the pinch, making their staff redundant. The never-had-it-so-good years were coming to an end. After a while he was offered a place at Max Rayner's studios, also in the West End, and for a time things started to buck up. But slowly Dad realised he could no longer maintain our five bedroom house on the money he was earning. We were forced to move to a three-bed semi, near the station in Bexley, but after only two years, money was running out again. He decided to make a clean break and invited an antique dealer to the house one Saturday while I was at work. They took all the artefacts and gave him a pittance for them. I was upset – I was sure I could've made a difference if he'd waited.'

'Did you know Mal then?'

I nod. 'We got married in 1970 and I was pregnant with Grace by the time Mum and Dad moved to Margate. That was late 71. They took an out-of-season holiday flat for six months while they looked for somewhere permanent to live. Then they were offered a council flat seventeen floors up in a tower block, Arlington House. It had a sea view but Dad sorely missed his garden. He had to make do with the many pots of geraniums he lovingly tended on the sideboard in the living room. There was still no work in his trade so he found a job gardening in the municipal parks and thought it would give him a chance to put his horticultural knowledge to good use.'

'Yeah, that's what I'm looking forward to – putting my knowledge of twenty years in the music industry to good use. Sorry, go on.'

'Anyway, they treated him more like a labourer. The money was poor and he felt useless. He used to know the Latin names of all the plants in our garden.'

'Yeah, I remember that garden in Bexley. It was stunning. And your mum?'

'Mum got a job at the Sea-Bathing hospital and took on extra cleaning jobs to help out but it still wasn't enough. I found out later from Herbie there had been terrible rows over money.'

Ron squeezes my hand. 'You OK? Do want to carry on?'

I nod again. 'It's all right. I need to talk it out.' I took a sip of my drink, and breathed. 'Well, on this particular Sunday in April, we arrive at ten-thirty to find Dad on his own and a bit surprised that we're early. He looked a bit put out but made us a pot of tea. He didn't have one himself – he had a drink poured out. Mum was at work at the hospital. Louise was home from university, working at the Winter Gardens box office. Herbie was in his bedroom. Grace asked for the colouring pencils – the usual ritual – and Dad took them out of the desk and gave them to her with some paper. She sat at the table and started to draw a birthday cake with candles on it. Dad showed her how to make it simple and drew one for her with his expert flourish. But he seemed preoccupied. He stared out the window at the cold grey sea. Drank his whisky, poured another and lit a cigarette. We made small talk until he said he was going downstairs to check the oil in the car and maybe get some petrol. We thought nothing of it, said we'd see him later.'

Breathe. I can feel my heart racing.

Ron gave my hand another squeeze. 'You don't have to do this.'

'I do. I've got to finish now I've started.'

'You sure?'

I nod again. 'Well, Dad was a long time and we wondered where he'd got to. Louise came in and suggested we go down to the bar along the sea front to see if he was waiting for us. He'd done this before so it seemed feasible. Mum came in and started cooking the dinner. Herbie was still in his bedroom. Louise, Mal and I left Grace in the flat, still drawing, and went down in the lift.

'But Dad wasn't there. We had a couple of drinks and waited. We all started speculating about what had happened then Herbie

140

bursts through the door and walks over to us, eyes staring straight ahead.

'Mum said can you come back upstairs?' We all look at each other. We ask what's happened but he can't answer. He just walks out and we all follow him into the lift.

'Mal blurts out, 'I hope he hasn't broken down somewhere. That old banger's past its best!'

Ron nods and waits for the rest.

'I look at Herbie – nothing. The lift doors open and something is mentioned about Dad probably being in the flat all along, waiting for us.

'The door to 17G is open. Two police officers, a man and a woman, are standing in the living room. My heart drops into my stomach and my heart thumps against my ribs. Mum comes out of the kitchen and we all look at each other until the policewoman says, 'Shall I tell them?'

'Mum nods.

'What?' I said, 'What is it?'

'The police woman looks at me. 'I'm afraid your father 's been found drowned in the harbour... he's...they tried...'

'I didn't hear the rest. I shouted, 'NO! NO! HE CAN'T BE! He can't be...' Mal tried to comfort me but I beat his chest with my fists, my whole body heaving, hot tears soaking his shirt. I didn't want the two police officers staring at me. My father was dead. I couldn't believe I'd never see him again. Still can't. I wanted to crawl into a hole and never come out.

' Julie, you don't have to go on with this.'

'No, I want to. I need to.'

Ron sighs. Takes a gulp of his drink.

'Anyway, when I come out of my stupor the police have gone. Mum carries on as normal, if nothing's happened.

'I don't know who's going to eat this chicken,' she says, and starts making sandwiches. Grace is still drawing at the table; amidst all the confusion everyone has forgotten about her. I don't want her to see me like that so I run to the bathroom and lock the door to be alone with my grief.'

I wipe my eyes. Ron cuddles me to him. But I'm there, back in 1977. 'Snatches of conversation later implied that Dad had driven down to the harbour and left the car there. Someone, an anaesthetist, had been sailing his yacht at the time and noticed a man in the water. He dialled 999 and they managed to drag him out. They took him to hospital and tried to resuscitate him but he wasn't responding. Someone suggested he had lost the will to live. Mal went to the hospital with Mum to identify the body. I clung to a glimmer of hope that they'd made a terrible mistake. But of course, they hadn't.'

'Maybe it was a cry for help that went wrong?' asked Ron.

'I don't know. Mum said he'd tried it before – he came home soaking wet one evening. Also, he'd taken to drinking heavily to give him Dutch courage. I knew nothing about this. If only...'

'Sshh. We're all wise after the event. It's no use speculating.'

Silent now, I remain cuddled up to Ron remembering the weeks that followed. I lived every day on automatic pilot. The light of my life had been snuffed out. I felt numb. I tried to find a way to deal with my grief and immersed myself in my work. My customers were all very sympathetic and one of them even suggested I view it as though my dad had gone to live in Australia.

'How old was your dad?' asks Ron, gently.

I blow my nose and wipe my eyes. 'Only fifty-eight.' Hot unstoppable tears burst forth afresh.

He holds me close and tries to comfort me just as Mal did all those years ago. It's not enough. It will never be enough. The death of my father has left a big black gaping hole that can never be filled.

'Yeah,' he says, 'I worry about those two down there,' pointing in the direction of Lottie and Jack's. 'That's another reason I came back. So I can keep an eye on them.'

Ron gets up and pours me another gin and tonic. He dishes up the dinner but I've lost what appetite I had. Again he compliments me on being good on the fang, but I eat because I have to and don't want to appear ungrateful.

Now I've reopened that dreadful wound, I find it difficult to stitch it back up. I think of all the words to describe my father: unique, artistic, gentle, and colourful. Dead. This last one doesn't belong; it's ugly, and black as the shiny hearse entering the cemetery, waiting. Waiting for the little chapel of rest to receive the coffin. The day is cold and grey. I am sitting in the car behind with Mal and his mother. I resent her presence. I focus on the hearse in front idling; the exhaust fumes escaping into the cold air. Waiting seems like an eternity. It's not possible that my dad is in that coffin in that vehicle – it must be somebody else. The service goes past me in a blur of tears. We follow the hearse to where a six-foot hole has been dug in readiness, fake grass covering the earth. I stand watching the coffin being taken out of the vehicle. Cold reality suddenly hits me as I see the brass nameplate. It *is* my dad. I watch the coffin being lowered into its final resting place. Uncontrollable heaving sobs wrack my body, like an alien struggling to burst out of my chest. I wonder where that horrible noise is coming from then realise it's me. Mal, steady as a rock, holds onto me for fear I will collapse. I feel empty and desolate and as if I'm sinking into the damp ground. My mother looks on, as if it's someone else's funeral. My brother and sister look at me with alarm; they are both composed. I just want to be left alone with my dad. But he is in that cold unwelcoming ground. I hear the thud of earth on the coffin, soon to be covered forever.

Back at the flat, all I can do is gaze out the window into a bleak and unrelenting future without the one person I revere above all others.

Ron brings me back to the present, reaches across the table, his warm hand on mine. He smiles. My heart flutters. His is a smile that says how sorry he is that I haven't been able to express my grief before or come to terms with it. We finish the meal in silence.

Ron's a very caring person so why can't I relax with him? Maybe he's going too fast for me? Perhaps I need some time on my own? I'm not used to another person continually in my space – I'm beginning to feel claustrophobic.

I look into his eyes, full of warmth and sympathy. He smiles again and I feel guilty for having these thoughts.

After dinner, we take another drink out into the garden. Alcohol always loosens the tongue, and we come to the conclusion that I should go home tomorrow for one night. The house is empty and it will give me some breathing space and time to clear my head.

'And another thing,' Ron says, 'I don't want you driving on that M25. Leave your car here and take the train. That way I'll be a lot happier. I don't want you driving with such a lot on your mind.'

WEDNESDAY 27 MAY 1987

Ron and I walk down to Lottie and Jack's to tell them what I'm doing.

Jack smiles, 'You are coming back though, aren't you? There'll be a row if you don't!'

'Of course! Try keeping me away.'

They're such nice people, they so obviously want our relationship to work that I feel the pressure keenly. Ron carries my overnight bag and escorts me to the station. I look around remembering the last time I was here in 1966. Nothing and everything has changed.

He sees me onto the train then walks alongside, trying to keep pace with it, smiling at me all the time then it slowly leaves him behind. I wave him goodbye and his image dissolves along with my nervous tension.

Warmed by the sun coming through the window I relax into a doze. I enjoy being on the move; motion of any kind always soothes me. Even walking lubricates the mind, oils the cogs. I can think more clearly.

I feel so different away from Ron. I'm surprised he's so possessive, so different to what he was twenty years ago. Then, he always spoke of freedom, now, ironically, it's me who craves freedom. Between Petersfield and Waterloo I analyse the situation and hope it all resolves once he's got a job. I know he's anxious about this and it's one of the reasons why we can't totally relax with each other. Added to this, I am rigid with the terrible guilt for what I've left behind. It weighs me down.

After three hours and a change at King's Cross, my train pulls into Royston station. I ring Pauline to collect me – she's going to lend me her car – but she's had a drink, and Arthur, her partner, is 'unavailable'. So I ring for a taxi to take me to Great Chishill.

Pauline opens the door. 'Come on in and tell me all your news! I've got a bottle of champagne on ice, if there's something to celebrate?' she looks straight at me with her brown eagle eyes. 'It is good news, I hope?'

'I just need someone to talk to.'

I sit down in her pale green and cream living room with the sun streaming in through the bay window, showing up the stains on the carpet. I mentally start to make patterns in them. She goes to the kitchen and comes back with a glass of bubbly.

'Here you are.' She stares at me. 'You know what I think?' she tosses her head dramatically and lights a cigarette, blows the smoke up to the ceiling. 'I think you need more time. You don't know if you're on your head or your heels at the moment.'

A sip of ice-cold champagne hits my empty stomach with a jolt.

Her eyes never leave me; I'm in the dock. 'Why don't you come and live here? I won't ask you for any rent just do my hair for nothing. When Mal comes back he'll expect you to make a move. This way, it'll give you time to come to the right decision.'

It's very tempting and she's obviously given it a lot of thought, but living with Pauline? Her ways are so different to mine and there's something lying under the surface that makes me uncomfortable. She seems to swing from one emotion to another aided by alcohol.

'Ron can come and stay at weekends; you need a stop gap.'

But how can I tell him this?

Ron phones. More pressure. Why can't he leave me alone? I tell him what Pauline has proposed. He seems happy about it but I don't think he's properly taken it on board.

Pauline tells me to take her car and bring it back tomorrow – Arthur will drive me to the station in the morning.

The stale smell hits me as I sit in Pauline's old Mazda; there are empty plastic drinks bottles rolling around under the seats, old sweet wrappers and crisp packets on the floor and on the back seat. The ashtray so full it won't close. The petrol gauge is almost on empty. I hate being without my car, dependent on other people. I feel stranded and wish Ron hadn't persuaded me to take the train.

I let myself in. It feels all wrong, like I'm a squatter in my own home. I hope the neighbours haven't noticed the old banger on the drive but I've parked it well back off the road, between our house and next door. I'm gagging for a cup of tea but there's no milk in the fridge. As I walk down the empty lane I have to stop myself breaking into a skip like a child coming home from school. I buy a frozen curry and a pint of milk in the Spar shop and come straight home. Luckily, I haven't bumped into anyone I know: I'm not in the mood to explain. I come in and shut out the world.

Yes! Sanctuary, albeit for one night.

I feel my shoulders relax but it's silent as a morgue – Soot's at the cattery, so I don't even have him for company. Guilt rears its ugly head again and I wonder how they're getting on in Menorca, and if Grace is enjoying herself, in spite of the circumstances.

On impulse I go upstairs to her bedroom. I can feel her energy impregnated on the space. Duran Duran and Madonna LPs on the floor next to her record player, one record left on the turntable. School books in an untidy heap on the floor, artwork scattered about. Hair and make-up products on her dressing table amongst the dust because she refuses to let me touch anything. I sit on her bed and pick up her Teddy. An image of Mum giving him to her as a baby unfolds before me.

The birth of a first baby is supposed to be a happy occasion but I still feel robbed of that.

We were living with Mal's parents in their Dickensian two-bedroom council flat in Camberwell at the time, having been evicted from the flat above the shop where I worked. I wasn't allowed tenancy once I ceased working for my boss (who was also my landlord)I couldn't carry on working as I had no one to look after the baby. We were unable to buy a house because we couldn't get a mortgage on Mal's wage alone – he only earned £32 a week.

I begrudged having to share the two-bedroom flat with my dominating in-laws. The area was alien to me and I longed for home, but Mum and Dad were in the process of moving.

On the night Grace began to make her presence felt, I got up and went downstairs thinking I needed the toilet. I sat there for about twenty minutes unaware of what was happening. I didn't realise my waters were breaking at first. Then the pains started. I was scared stiff. I went upstairs and sat on the bed as quietly as I could and timed the contractions. I didn't want to wake Mal until I was sure.

I touched him on the arm. 'Wake up! We've got to go!'

'What? What's happening? Where we going?'

I rushed to get dressed and took my packed case from where it had been standing in readiness for weeks and urged him to get a move on.

Realisation dawned and he flapped about trying to find his socks, pants and the rest of his clothes, then a panic to find his car keys. He poked his head round his parents' bedroom door. 'We're off to the hospital!'

My contractions were coming every fifteen minutes. Then five minutes. I knew from the anti-natal classes that the birth was imminent.

We got to Dulwich maternity hospital at 4.am. A night nurse opened the door and took us upstairs in the lift. She asked me all the relevant questions and put me in a delivery room. Mal waited outside while they gave me an enema. I was frightened – I didn't know what was happening, what to expect. My body felt as though it was going to split wide open. They gave me pethedin for the pain but it did nothing. Then the gas and air mask was thrust over my face. I wanted Mal but he wasn't there. They wheeled me out into the labour ward and I heard a nurse say, 'She's about to have it. You can come in if you want?'

But Mal's voice said, 'No, that's alright. I'll wait here.' And my heart sank.

The last stage of labour was taking forever. The contractions were lessening. I was getting tired. Then I heard the big black midwife say to the little white trainee, 'Make an incision. Just there.'

I felt nothing but relief when the baby gushed out.

'It's a little girl. What are going to call her?'

'Grace.' I'd chosen the name months ago *knowing* I was going to have a little girl.

'That's a lovely name. I'm sure she'll be very graceful,' chuckled the black midwife, her heavy bosom shaking like a jelly.

They wrapped Grace in a pink blanket and laid her in my arms. But her dark blue eyes stared blankly at me and she screamed. Maybe she knew what was in store for her.

They took Grace away and left me lying on the trolley. I felt cold and lonely, exposed and nervous of the massive responsibility of caring for this new life. I was only twenty-two and unprepared for motherhood.

The midwife came back and forced my legs into two stirrups in readiness for the stitching. I don't remember if I felt any pain.

I learned later, when Mal went back to tell his parents I'd had a little girl, his father asked, 'You sure they haven't made a mistake, son?'

That hurt. I felt like Anne Boleyn unable to produce an heir.

We lived with Mal's granny in her terraced council house for the next four years. His mother and other relations all lived in the vicinity and took charge of Grace's upbringing. I felt powerless and alone but being young, I allowed it to happen. I regained my independence and went back to work, Mal's mother taking control. Consequently, over the years, I became disengaged from Grace.

We never had any more children. When Grace was three I thought I was pregnant again. Mal had a word with his cousin and bought a drink from the off-licence that was supposed to induce miscarriage. He said we couldn't afford any more kids.

'Here, drink this. It'll sort you out.'

I thought long and hard; I was in two minds. On the one hand I would've liked another baby, a playmate for Grace. On the other, I liked my freedom and was used to Mal's mother taking responsibility. And she made it very clear she wouldn't look after more than one baby. Also, I had fallen out of love with Mal and knowing how he felt, I wasn't prepared to find out if another baby could stitch us back together.

I drank the stuff. It was disgusting, like petrol. The following day I had bad stomach cramps and a heavy period. It had done its job.

Looking back, I feel cheated of what might have been and guilty for not being more assertive. And now, added to this is my newly pressed guilt.

I go back downstairs, put the curry in the oven and make a cup of tea. I don't know why, but I phone Ron.

He starts giggling. 'It sounded as though she'd had a few!'

'Oh, Pauline? Yeah, more than a few, I think!' My voice sounds overloud in the empty house.

'You sound happy.'

'Yeah, I think I'm doing the right thing living with Pauline for a while. It just gives me some breathing space.'

'OK, I'll ring you in the morning before you come back. I love you. Can't wait to see you again. I'm missing you already.'

He's pressuring me again and I know he's ignored Pauline's suggestion. But for now, I'm going to enjoy the peace and solitude of being in the house on my own.

After my curry and another cup of tea, I ring Herbie. He tells me Mum has gone into hospital today for an intrusive X-ray. More guilt on my overloaded shoulders but he assures me she's doing well.

He picks up on my mood. 'Are you all right? You sound very nervy.'

I don't want to worry him. 'Yeah, I think so.'

'Keep your chin up. You can phone anytime for a chat, you know.'

'I know. Thanks. I'll be OK'

After a glass of wine it occurs to me that Ron seems to live at such a fast pace, as if he's trying to fit everything into the time he has left. I hope I'm wrong.

I switch on the television for background noise, write my diary and have another glass of wine. I go to bed at ten, in the spare room – I can't bring myself to sleep in the marital bed. Can't even go into that room; it's nothing to do with me anymore. Totally exhausted, I'm asleep as soon as my head touches the pillow.

THURSDAY 28 MAY 1987

I wake refreshed from a dreamless sleep, the best I've had for weeks. As I eat my breakfast the sun is shining on the sadly neglected garden. The once loved, manicured lawns and colourful boarders need attention and I silently berate Mal for wallowing in his self-pity and apathy.

I'm getting ready for my return to Petersfield, putting the last touches to my hair and make-up, lost in my thoughts when the phone makes me jump.

'I just phoned to say I love you. Have a good journey back. I'm just going out to get the shopping. Do you like steak and kidney?' He barely gives me a chance to answer. 'I'll have the dinner on when you get back. I'll meet you from the station. See you soon. Love you.'

I'm torn between another day to myself and hurrying back to Ron. I just hope I feel more relaxed over the next few days.

I take the car back to Pauline's. With a sinking heart I hear that Arthur is 'unavailable' again. She's still hung over but decides to drive me to Royston station stopping for petrol on the way. Time is running out. I know I'm going to miss my train but I don't want to appear ungrateful, so I say nothing.

Sure enough, I reach the station to find the train has left without me. I have an hour to wait for the next one. More time to analyse my situation. I do love Ron, but half of me wants to run away. Maybe when we've made love it'll all calm down?

The train comes rolling in and with it my resolve to face whatever comes my way. I have instigated this whole thing, after all. I'm wrapped up in my thoughts the whole journey and vow that I'll take control in the next few days and be more assertive. I have become a frightened little mouse and that's not like me.

The train rolls into Petersfield at one-thirty. Through the station doorway, I spot Ron on the other side of the road and my heart heaves with love for him. I have such a conflict of emotions; I hope Ron doesn't pick up on it. I walk through to meet him – he spots me and a big smile lights up his face. I sense his impatience as he waits for a break in the traffic. He finally runs across, takes my hand and gives me a big kiss. 'Did you miss your train?'

'Yeah, Pauline's fault.'

He seems anxious to get me home; takes long strides. 'Been waiting long?'

'No, only a couple of minutes.'

Back at the house, I suddenly feel very hungry and make myself a sandwich and a cup of tea. Ron doesn't want any; he's got a can of Foster's.

Ever since I've been with him, Ron's done everything in the house, and in my logic I decide to take more control, hoping I'll feel better. It works.

I sit and watch him sort through his resumes yet again and wonder if he's done anymore about looking for work.

He reads my mind.

'I rang a couple of agents yesterday. They want me to go and see them next week. Sounds hopeful.'

'Oh good.' I have to tell him that I need to be on my own sometimes; I'm not used to being with another person twenty-four hours a day, seven days a week. I brace myself, hoping he doesn't get the wrong impression.

'I've been thinking.'

He looks up from his paperwork. 'Yeah? What about?'

'It's just... I like a bit of space to myself now and then. Ever since I've been here, we seem to be together. But please don't take it the wrong way.'

He smiles. Always a good sign. 'Yeah, I know what you mean! I realise I've been a bit overpowering. Sorry. Somehow it just seems to happen, doesn't it?'

I nod.

'When I've finished here, I'll take you up on the heath. Let you see what it's like on a sunny day.'

Memories of that ill-fated night in 1966 flood my mind. I tentatively start to reminisce with Ron, leaving out the discomfort he put me through. But he barely remembers it. Or says he doesn't.

The blue sky and the clear air are liberating. There are families enjoying the good weather; playing ball, walking dogs. As we walk along the grassy bank, I slip my hand in his.

'Mmm,' he says, 'That's what I like, those little affectionate squeezes. Gives me reassurance.'

We take a boat out on the lake. Ron takes the oars expertly. I lean back, watching him, my hand hanging over the side, the cool water trickling through my fingers. He's in his element – he loves boats. He's had to sell his own to come back to England of course, and I begin to wonder if he's not more enamoured with boats than with me. He smiles at me and I quash the thought.

We moor the boat. He's anxious the dinner will spoil so we go home.

Ron pours me a gin and tonic and helps himself to another can of Foster's. We sit in the garden, talking. I never get bored with listening to him, but what he expects of this country is worrying. He's envisaged, rather vainly I feel, coming back to an England that welcomes him with open arms and gives him a job immediately.

He looks down at my hands. 'Dad noticed you're still wearing your wedding band,' he says, accusingly.

Oh, dear. I haven't given this much thought but after sixteen years I forget I've got it on.

'I'm sorry. I'll take it off. It's just...'

Ron shoots me one of his looks.

In the bathroom, I soap my finger to remove the ring but it leaves behind a deep indentation, mocking me.

I take my seat at the table. The meal looks delicious – stewed steak and kidney, mashed potatoes and green beans. He pours two glasses of Corbières, looks at my finger, and smiles.

We chink glasses and hold hands across the table. His eyes bore into my soul.

'Here's to us and our new life together. You've made me a very happy man this week. Thank you for sending me that fortieth birthday card.'

He squeezes my hand and a warm feeling spreads throughout my whole body. I know it's not the wine. He IS the person I want – he always has been and always will be.

I write in my diary – 'The best day I've spent with Ron. I love him very much. He's the only one for me. Didn't want the day to end. He's wonderful. I'M VERY HAPPY'.

But by the time we go to bed he is too drunk to seal our love.

FRIDAY 29 MAY 1987

Ron has made arrangements to stay with Robert and Madge on the Isle of Wight this evening and to pick up a rental car tomorrow. He takes control, looking very officious while he packs the overnight bag. But I have an uneasy feeling in the pit of my stomach as we set off for the train to Portsmouth.

Ron's eager for me to know everything about Australia and takes me first to the exhibition of Aboriginal Art in Portsmouth. He explains the Dreamtime paintings to me with their expressive swirls and dots, but his voice trails off. It's fascinating but I can't concentrate – something is nagging at the back of my mind.

From there he takes me to the First Fleet exhibition. This is all about the first settlers in January 1788. Whilst waiting in dock to depart, the conditions on board ship were horrendous and even worse on the journey. It was a wonder any of the convicts survived the voyage. The exhibition is very evocative – they've gone to a lot of trouble to reproduce the atmosphere of those times and we spend a good hour taking it all in. Nowadays it's unthinkable that a young girl could be deported for stealing a table cloth and the thought sends a shiver through me. Next January will be the bi-centennial of course, and Australia is gearing up for the celebrations. January – my thirty-ninth birthday. My mind is racing ahead.

Ron drags me back to the present. 'Do you want to see the Mary Rose?'

'I'd love to. Is it far?'

'No, just a bit more walking, that's all.'

We have done a lot of walking already but we resolutely join the queue in which we stand for thirty minutes. In the hallway is a display case with *Driza-Bone* rainwear. Ron tells me they're an Australian company and they're brilliant at what they do – it seems everything in Australia is brilliant. When we finally go in to see the Mary Rose, Henry VIII's flagship, the only part on show is the hull. I remember watching it on television three years ago being lifted out of the sea. Now, it's continually being sprayed with sea water to preserve it. The fact that it's so old is amazing but I have to exercise a lot of imagination to realise the size of the whole ship. There are also some original Tudor canons in the exhibition; Ron has a dreamy expression as he lays his hands on one of them. He looks as though he's trying to pick up the energy from the ancient relic, soaking up the passing of time.

How amazing – no one I know has ever done this.

On our way out from the harbour we pass The Victory, the black and yellow windows at its stern impressively towering above us. I imagine Nelson in there, but Ron realises we've done enough sightseeing by this time and decides to give it a miss. I'm relieved. I'm feeling rather weary.

At five-thirty we meet Robert and Madge who have separate businesses in Portsmouth. They still look the same as they did twenty years ago. Happy smiling faces and hugs all round. All four of us take the train to the passenger ferry. While we're on board we see the impressive sights of the Ark Royal and the QE2 in the Solent. It's been an amazing day.

Next, there's a surprise in store: the train that takes us to Brading is an old London underground train.

Ron smiles at me. 'We probably travelled on this very train all those years ago! 1966 eh?'

This gives me goose-bumps – something from *our* past is with us today.

Ron's nephew, Paul, is waiting to pick us up at the station. He drives us all to Robert and Madge's bungalow – a lovely place in its own grounds – then he leaves. Madge makes us all a cup of tea, then she suggests we all go to the leisure centre for an evening meal. I begin to hope I can eat it – I feel a bit sick and shell-shocked by the day's events.

Ron and Robert go to the counter to order the meal while Madge sits with me. She's eager to hear of all the events leading up to today. Her smiles tell me how amazing she thinks it all is, especially our first meeting in Trafalgar Square.

The leisure centre is part of Tesco's busy complex. The name is mocking me again – it seems there's always something to remind me. Madge is not surprised when I tell her that my husband works for Tesco's, but I feel uneasy and try to keep my guilt from rising to the surface.

The meal finally arrives but I have no appetite. The echoing noise in the complex muffles all conversation between Ron, Madge and Robert. They sink into the distance while I sink into myself. The tight feeling in my belly is getting worse, like a vice grip. Panic sets in that I might actually be sick. I run to the loo. Madge follows me. As soon as I'm in the cubicle I realise I have a problem – my period is early and I have nothing with me. Damn. That's all I need; now what am I going to do? I sit with my head in my hands trying to think. I come out of the cubicle and see Madge on her own, washing her hands.

'Ah, Madge?'

She looks round.

'I've got a bit of a problem... I've come on and I've got nothing with me.'

She smiles. 'Oh, isn't it always the way? Don't worry, I'll ask Robert to stop at the shop on the way back.'

'Oh, thanks,' I breathe. 'I just wasn't expecting it.'

'No problem.'

By the time we pile into the car Ron is the worse for drink. He keeps giggling. 'Where are we going? Is it a surprise?' He asks, while Robert makes a detour to the shop. I keep quiet. Robert stops the car and Madge gets out and runs into the general store. She's back in a flash and hands me a newspaper with a packet of sanitary towels hidden inside. I hug them to me as if my life depends on them. When we arrive at the bungalow I rush to the loo and wonder what other problems will befall me.

Later, when we go to bed, I tell Ron what's happened. His face clouds over and he puts his arms round me.

'Oh, my poor little Vegimite! Are you OK?'

This has become his pet name for me; apparently, there is a rather watered down Australian version of our Marmite. The television adverts are current, although I have never seen them.

I nod. 'Yeah, I'll be fine now.'

'You sure? I know some women have terrible trouble with that.'

'Luckily I'm not one of them.'

We get into bed and Ron soon falls into a heavy sleep while I lay awake for hours.

SATURDAY 30 MAY 1987

I awake to the sun streaming in through a crack in the curtains and remember the difficulty I was in the night before. I run to the en suite. Still in a sound sleep, Ron is oblivious to any of my movements.

I luxuriate in the water running over my body and take my time. My mind is galloping ahead but I try to think positive – Ron's word. He uses it a lot. I sit on the bed to dry my hair and the noise of the hairdryer wakes him. He smiles sleepily at me, propping his head up on one arm.

'How's my little Vegemite?'

I turn off the hairdryer, lean across and kiss his bed-warm lips. 'I'm fine.'

He looks relieved. 'Mm, I suppose I ought to get in there.' He suddenly jumps out of bed with renewed vigour, into the en-suite, and I'm amazed that he can change that quickly.

The wonderful aroma of breakfast greets me when I enter the kitchen. Madge looks up from the bacon and eggs she's cooking and smiles. 'All right?'

'Better now, thanks Madge.'

'There's a pot of tea on the table, Julie. Help yourself. Where's Ron?'

I sense his presence behind me, even before I hear his voice.

'I'm never far away when there's food about, you should know that!' He puts his arms round me and places his warm lips on my neck. Madge smiles.

There's a 'Good morning,' from Robert who glances at the paper while we all sit round the big pine table. I'm suddenly ravenous. Madge has gone to a lot of trouble – a full cooked breakfast, toast and marmalade, like a hotel. Ron and Robert discuss their plans to pick up the hire car and joke that its probably one mark short of 'Rent-a-Wreck' but it'll do. After breakfast I start to help Madge clear away but she won't hear of it. 'No, it's fine, Julie. Go and sit in the garden. Take the paper.'

This is obviously a big part of their daily routine; they all seem very interested in the daily news and very clued up on local events. And they never miss a trick where business opportunities are concerned. All three – Robert, Madge and Sally – have their own businesses. I should have plenty of support when I start mine.

Ron goes to pick up the hire car with Robert, while I lay back on the lounger on the sun-drenched patio. I watch Madge as she waters the colourful bedding plants in the raised beds, then she comes to chat.

'You've made a huge difference to Ron – he seems really contented since he's come back.'

'Yes, it's like a dream come true for both of us. But I think he's a bit anxious about getting a good job.'

'Early days. Robert will be able to point him in the right direction, if he needs it,' she says, confidently.

I am relieved. The whole family are lovely, they all help each other and I have the feeling my new life will be amazing.

Madge looks in the direction of the door and goes to make Ron and Robert, who have returned, a cup of tea. Ron's got a surprise for me – he's dug out his old guitar and bought some new strings. He sits on the low wall and proceeds to restring the instrument, a cup of tea by his side. He starts to play and smiles at me as he sings: *Let me take you by the hand and lead you through the streets of London....* my yearning and love for the nineteen-year-old Ron fill me up.

He stops abruptly, carefully leans his guitar against the wall. 'Come on. I'll show you the sights!' he takes me by the hand and leads me to the car shouting over his shoulder, 'See you later, Madge!'

She smiles at us both. 'Of, course. Enjoy yourselves!'

Glimpses of calm turquoise sea come into view as we round the different headlands. He stops the car near Freshwater and we get out to take in the view. He takes my hand.

'No walking today, Julie Ann,' he smiles. 'I just wanted you to see this.'

He leads me to a gap in the hedge high up on a cliff top. A wide bay opens out before us, the sun sparkles like a million diamonds on the waves that gently roll in. The huge expanse of bleached white sand seems to go on forever. We stand breathing in the ozone, bathed in warmth and each other, and I feel totally alive.

'Beautiful, isn't it?' He gently tilts my face up to his and kisses me. 'So are you.'

Arms round each other, I feel at this moment, that I should never have to worry again or have any doubts about my love for Ron. I feel complete. Whatever obstacle comes up, we'll tackle it together.

He leads me through the gap in the hedge and down some steep narrow steps. They are uneven so I have to walk behind him. He looks round at me. 'You OK?'

I nod and carefully pick my way through the brambles, holding onto his strong hand. We finally draw level with the beach. I jump the last two steps into the soft sand and breathe in the view. 'Wow!'

'I knew you'd like it.'

It seems we have it to ourselves. We run and skip along the wet sand like a couple of kids. Ron stops near the water's edge and picks up a flat pebble. 'How are you at skimming?'

I have to confess I've never mastered the art. He takes aim. The pebble skims the water, jumps three or four times then plops into the sea leaving ever-increasing ripples.

'You try. Here. Like this.'

He repeats his party trick. I watch then go hunting for a suitable pebble. I feel curiously child-like until memories of days out with Grace and Mal in Margate invade my thoughts.

Ron shouts. 'Found one?' The tail end of his voice drifts on the wind.

I nod. I pick up the big flat purple pebble and start to take aim, remembering Mal doing the same. Ron runs over to me. 'Ha! That one's too big! Here.' He gives me another.

'OK, here goes.' I toss the pebble into the sea. It bounces once then makes a giant plop. A vision of Mal shaking his head swims in front of me. 'Told you,' I shout. 'I'm useless.'

'No! You're not useless. It's not important.' Ron grabs my hand and pulls me up the beach and we sit on the warm dry sand. He looks at his watch. 'We'll go in a minute.'

I pick up a handful of dry powdery sand and watch it drift through my fingers and into the wind, my mind on Mal and Grace, wondering if they have enjoyed Menorca. Ron puts his hand over mine forcing it down. 'Don't do that. It makes you look sad.' The sea is reflected in his pale eyes and I'm reminded of *Your Wildest Dreams* again.

'I love you, Julie Ann.'

'I love you, too.'

His eyes are full of love; the cloudless sky behind him. I commit the picture to memory but he shatters the moment.

'Come on.' He helps me up and we climb back up to where the car is parked. He looks around and spots a tea room overlooking the bay. We're the only ones making use of the white plastic table and chairs in the sunshine. A waitress comes out to take our order and Ron says he'd like a cream tea.

'But it's lunchtime,' I point out.

'That's OK, I'll have lunch later!'

I shake my head in mock dismay. I decide on a tuna and salad sandwich and a cup of tea.

'Yeah,' says Ron, 'make that two. I was only joking about the cream tea.'

I tap him playfully on the arm. 'What am I gonna do with you?'

He answers me with a lecherous grin and I wonder if he will ever fulfil his intentions. It won't happen now my body has decided otherwise, and I'm going home tomorrow. But I can't bring myself to think about that. Not now.

The waitress comes back with our order and we sit in complete harmony enjoying the food and watching the yachts in the distance. They remind me of what Ron has given up. I push the thought away. 'I've always wanted a tea room,' I blurt out.

Ron looks up from his plate. 'There's no reason why not. I think you'd be good at it. Yeah, I can see it now,' he draws in the air, *'Julie's Tea Room.* Very English!'

'I'm serious.'

'OK, so am I. Where do you propose to open this tea room?'

I shrug. 'Dunno. I'd have to do some research.'

'Well, the first thing is dreaming about it, then you start working towards it, it becomes practical and becomes achievable,' he says, with conviction.

Plans are starting to form in my mind but it's all going too fast for me again. Ron's like that; as soon as something presents itself he runs with it and sees it through to the end. It's his star sign – Sagittarius – his mantra is 'don't think about it, do it'. I'm a more cautious Aquarian.

'Have you got the money? If not, I'm sure we could talk to Sally.'

But it sounds wrong – for me to come in, an outsider whom they know very little about and to rely on his family to help with finance.

I shake my head. 'I'll have to look into it.'

No more is said.

On the way back to the bungalow my mind is stretching ahead with all the plans Ron and I will be making, where we'll be living and if I will open a tea room. It's always been a dream of mine but I can't see any further than tomorrow at the moment.

Back at Robert and Madge's bungalow, after a convivial dinner of roast chicken and all the trimmings, we say our goodbyes. Robert and Madge have made us very welcome and I only hope I have conveyed my thanks enough for the last two days – I'm looking forward to many more like this.

Sitting in the queue waiting to board the ferry, Ron turns to me. 'I love you, Julie Ann.' He picks up my hand and kisses it.

'I love you too, Ronald Edward.'

We are lost in each other. The interior of the car, the sounds outside, all disappear, until a frantic car horn urges us to get going. We keep smiling at each other as Ron drives onto the ferry and parks the car expertly in the line.

Home at ten and I realise I should phone my mum after the ordeal of the intrusive X-ray on Wednesday. Ron pours me a gin and tonic while I dial the number. Mum sounds relieved it's all over and then surprises me by asking about Mal and Grace.

'Will they be back from their holiday by now?'

'Yes, they came home today. Will you do me a favour?'

'What's that?'

'Would you phone and ask if they had a good time? I don't think I can at the moment, but I'll be seeing them tomorrow; I've got to go home and sort things out.'

She sounds vague. 'Oh. Yes, all right, then.'

Although I know I should, I really can't bring myself to phone Mal tonight; it will ruin the whole day if he makes me feel guilty again. Ron says it's up to me, but he's concerned for Grace. I tell him I'll ring in the morning.

We have a happy evening. I ask Ron to play the *Wildest Dreams* video again. We argue good-naturedly about the car in the film.

'It's an old Ford Consul mark two,' I know I'm right.

'No, it's a Cortina.'

'No! Look at the headlamp!'

He winds it back and studies it again. 'OK, you win! How come you know so much about makes and models of cars?'

'I don't know; I've always taken an interest. I used to watch all the cars on the road when Dad first bought his Anglia. We used to discuss them.' The memory of Earl's Court motor show rises up. 'Did you ever get that sports car?'

He looks puzzled. 'What sports car?' Then it dawns on him. 'Oh, that one... nope, bought a boat instead!'

SUNDAY 31 MAY 1987

I woke up with Mal and Grace on my mind this morning. I realise now that I should've rung last night. I pick up the phone, take a deep breath and dial the number.

My fears are not unfounded.

'Grace was very upset when we got back last night to find you not there. It really upset me. She sat with your present in her lap and cried. How could you do that?'

A heavy lump falls into my stomach. 'Oh dear. I'm sorry, but I thought you knew I wouldn't be there until tonight?'

'It's not good enough. You just don't care!'

'No, it's not like that. I do care.'

'No, you don't.' He slams the phone down.

I feel despair swamping me again.

Ron takes me in his strong arms. 'Try not to worry. Remember – my inner strength is your inner strength. We've come this far; the rest should be easy.'

Why don't I believe him?

He makes breakfast and we have a lazy morning. Later, we walk down to the Harrow Inn, another lovely old country pub. We sit in the garden with our Foster's and I try to steady my nerves. I can feel Mal and Grace pulling me back; I should be on my way.

We go round to Lottie and Jack's for Sunday lunch. Lottie's cooked Ron's favourite, roast lamb, but I have no appetite. Every mouthful turns to string.

'When are you coming back, love?' asks Lottie.

My heart beats against my ribs. 'As soon as everything's sorted out – I still have all my customers to organise and the paperwork, letters to write...'

She nods but makes me feel I'm not making much effort.

At 2.45pm I leave for Melbourn and reassure Ron I'll soon be back.

'OK. Now, remember – you've got to be gentle with Grace. I feel for that poor little lady. Keep me posted next week and let me know how things work out.'

'Of course,' I blow out as deep breath. 'I'm not looking forward to this.'

'I know, but remember what I said. Inner strength. Just a few more hurdles.'

I kiss him goodbye and get in the car. As I pull off the drive, my body feels weighed down by what's waiting for me.

The journey is made longer by the fact that instead of turning left onto the M25, I end up going the long way round anti-clockwise, through the Dartford tunnel.

What's wrong with me? Why did I do that?

The whole journey I worry about whether I have enough petrol and what I'll find when I get there.

At five-thirty I pull onto the drive with a sniff of petrol to spare. I go straight to Grace and put my arms round her.

'Oh dear, I'm so sorry I wasn't here for you last night.'

She shrugs me off. I feel a fraud. I want to cry. After a week the gulf between us seems even wider. I stand, helpless in her sadness, and look down at my feet; feet that took me out of their lives and have no place back here.

I leave her and go downstairs. Mal looks up from the armchair as I enter the room, desperation written all over his face. I can feel the frown deepening across my brow.

So much pain still here. I had hoped it would be easier than this.

I speak first. 'I'm sorry...'

'It hasn't been easy. Steve had problems with Rose while we were away. He thought at one point that he was in with a chance to get it back together. The holiday's done nothing for me – in fact it's set me back a fortnight.'

I go to the kitchen and boil a kettle. Sharing tea might help. I don't want to be here. And I don't want to hear about the so-called holiday, but Ron's at my shoulder.

My inner strength....

Mal comes into the kitchen. 'Oh, Ju. You should've seen her last night.'

I pour the water in the pot. I can't look at him.

'She was so looking forward to giving you her present, and when she knew you weren't here she sat with it on her lap and burst into tears. It tore me apart.'

I should have been here. It was a bad mistake.

He reaches out then retracts his hand as if I've scolded him.

'All I ask is that I can lean on you. You're the only friend I've got. You're lucky; you've got someone who loves you and gives you that strength. I've got no one to turn to.' He looks down at his hands. 'You're the hub of it all; everyone loves you.'

I pour the tea and hand him one. We take it into the lounge. I feel for him, but on the other hand, I can't tear myself in two. I only hope he's not going to try and appeal to my better nature, yet again.

'If you're there when I need you, it would make me feel a lot easier about Grace. I don't want to try and get you in bed, nothing like that. It's finished, I know that. Just be there as a friend.'

'Of course.'

Phew. I wasn't expecting that.

We sit in silence. I wonder if Grace has heard any of our conversation. I go into the hall, glance up the stairs and notice her bedroom door is closed. I pull the lounge door to and ring Ron. I still feel awkward doing this with Mal in the next room but I try to put on a cheery voice. 'Well, I'm here but I had an awful journey.'

'Why?'

'I was nearly out of petrol and I took a wrong turn onto the M25. I had to go all the way round, anti-clockwise.'

'Ha! Silly bugger!'

'I know.'

I can feel he wants to ask about Grace and Mal. I get in first. 'Oh, dear. Poor Grace...'

Ron breaths down the phone and swallows. 'I told you, you have to treat her gently. Let me know how it goes over the next few days. Remember. Inner strength.'

'I love you. Speak to you soon.'

I don't want to go back in the lounge and I don't want to be with Grace. There's only one place to go. I take my bag up to the spare room and close the door.

MONDAY 1 JUNE 1987

I wake up with thoughts of all that I have to do today – start putting all my affairs in order before I finally go back to Petersfield for good. Now I'm here, what I'm doing seems unreal, as if I'm living two lives – one real and one imaginary.

With a heavy heart I see Grace off to school. She won't look me in the eye and I wonder if our relationship will ever recover. I sit with a cup of tea, making a list of all the customers that I won't be seeing this week, to tell them I'm leaving.

Mal doesn't go to work – instead he goes to see his solicitor. While he's out, I write the letter to my customers and make an appointment to see my accountant in Cambridge on Wednesday. Two positive steps. I ring Ron, hoping to please him. But he brushes it aside – he's been busy in the house, cleaned the bathroom and turned the bed round to face the window. 'I've got an interview on Wednesday for K-Tel. Sounds good. I've also been after another job that could turn out to be world-wide, so that's hopeful.'

World-wide?

'Great. I hope you have more luck this time. I'm missing you.'

'Yeah, you too.'

'I could've seen you at the weekend but Mal's gotta work so I'll have to stay with Grace.'

'Yeah, that's a shame.'

He doesn't sound too bothered. Maybe he thinks I'm not trying hard enough?

TUESDAY 2 JUNE 1987

I make an appointment to see my solicitor in Royston tomorrow afternoon; I need some advice on how to answer the letter from Mal's solicitor. Then I brace myself and go next door to ask Susan if she'll type the letter to my customers for me. I haven't seen her since the trouble started and I don't know what she'll think of me.

'Of course, no problem,' smiles Susan and stands to one side to let me in.

I'm relieved. 'Oh good, then I can get it photocopied and send it to all my customers; it'll be a lot cheaper than phone calls.' I rattle off.

Susan goes to put the kettle on. I follow her.

'How are you, Julie?'

The leading question.

'Oh,' I breathe, 'not bad. It's been a bit traumatic but I think the worst is over.'

Susan gestures for me to sit at the table, looks intently at me. 'Colin and I want you to know that we don't think any less of you as a person for what's happened.'

I feel my body relax. 'Oh, that's nice of you.'

'No, I mean it. These things happen in all families.'

'Well, it's very nice of you to say so. It's more difficult while I'm here but hopefully, I'll sort it out. I've just got to be strong.'

'Yes. It can't be easy. How's Grace?'

How indeed.

'I don't really know, she won't talk to me. I think that's the most difficult thing of all to deal with.'

'Yes, it must be very hurtful. If there's anything we can do, Julie, just say.'

'Thanks.'

Susan goes back to her kitchen and pours me a cup of tea. I glance around at their lounge, being the other half of the semi it's the opposite way round to ours. Everything looks the same as it always has, nothing's changed, but it feels different. Then I realise it's me that's changed. She comes back and hands me the tea and places a coaster on the table. I drink it while she types. She's a podgy little woman in her late twenties, married to Colin, an electrician. They have two girls – ten and three. Mal doesn't think they're the brightest of people. He criticises them for their simple ways, but at least they're happy.

Susan hands me the typed letter.

'Thanks, Susan. How much do I owe you?'

She shakes her head. 'That's all right, Julie. And don't forget, anytime you need to talk...'

'Thanks. You're very kind.'

I go back indoors and ring Ron to tell him of my progress, but he has friends round and sounds like he's been drinking. 'I wanna see you soon,' he slurs.

'Yes, I know, but I told you – it's difficult. Mal's working at the weekend.'

'Can't you get away tomorrow? I could meet you somewhere in London.'

'No, I can't. I've got too much to do. I've got to see the solicitor and the accountant and get things tied up for when I come back.'

One minute he's telling me to be careful with Grace and the next...

'Oh. OK.' He sounds disappointed. 'I wish I could help you.'

'So do I. It's not easy being away from you.'

A massive understatement.

'I hope the interview goes well tomorrow.'

'Yeah. I'll ring and let you know.'

I put the phone down and look forward to a bit of breathing space. Then Mal comes in. It's as if he knows Ron's been on the phone.

'Are you all right?' I ask. 'Is anything worrying you?'

He walks past me, muttering, 'It's just that I've never been murdered before.'

Anger starts to bubble up inside me. I hate being in the midst of all this melodramatic self-pity. Why can't he show a bit of strength for a change?

I get my accounts ready for tomorrow and begin to feel more positive. But I can't wait to be gone.

WEDNESDAY 3 JUNE 1987

Ron phones just before he's about to catch the train to London. He sounds very optimistic about the interview today. I wish him the best of luck and tell him I'll ring later.

Mal takes my letter to work with him to get it photocopied so I don't have to. He seems to swing from self-pity to being over-helpful and it's doing my head in.

First stop the bank to change my details, then on to the hairdressing wholesalers in Cambridge. The owner tells me I can still deal with him by post; he doesn't want to lose my custom. From there I go to see my accountant, also in Cambridge. He advises me to try and sell my business, at least get some money for the goodwill, but I can't see this happening – it's not like owning a shop.

I go back to Royston to the solicitor. Apparently, I can answer Mal's solicitor's letter without using him. Even better; more money saved. He tells me to stipulate that I want joint custody of Grace, meaning she still lives at the marital home with Mal, but I'll have a say in her education and how she's brought up. He tells me I need to ask for reasonable access – well, I can't imagine Mal will stop me entering the house – and tells me Mal should have 'care and control'. I should also stipulate I want a speedy divorce. This goes without saying. I should be released from all mortgages on the house, to transfer it all over to Mal in his name and no costs to be claimed from me. I'm happy to go along with this. I go straight back home and write the letter. All in all a very positive day; I feel I'm getting somewhere at last. I only hope Ron's had the same kind of experience.

Mal and Grace go out later so I take the opportunity to phone Ron. Expecting a favourable response, I tell him what I've been doing. But I'm greeted with his disappointing news.

'I haven't had much luck with a job, but I've made some useful contacts.'

'Oh, good,' I say, trying to keep him buoyed up.

'I'm going to London again tomorrow to look up some more people. If I haven't got a job by the time you come back, I'll be panicking.'

My heart starts thumping. 'Oh, dear. Try not to worry. I know it's easier said than done but I'm sure something will turn up.'

He blows a sigh down the phone. 'I hope you're right. I miss you. The house seems lonely without you. I want you back as soon as possible.'

'I know. I'm doing all I can. It won't be long now.'

FRIDAY 5 JUNE 1987

At 8:30am I ring Ron and get him out of bed. I can't believe it; he's always such an early bird. He tells me he didn't go to London yesterday. Instead, he wrote some letters and sent them out with his CV to various businesses. He's taking the car back to the Isle of Wight tomorrow – he can't afford to keep it any longer. He sounds fed up, not his usual up-beat self. Obviously he needs me there but I feel as if I'm being pulled in two again.

As I put down the receiver I notice the last three digits of our phone number are the same as Ron's first three – 61687 and 68792, and the year is 1987. 87 seems to be very prominent at the moment. Recurring numbers have always fascinated me and I wonder if this coincidence is significant.

In the evening, the atmosphere indoors is thick with tension and I'm relieved when Mal goes down the pub and Grace goes round to Claire's. When Mal comes back he pours himself a large whisky and slumps in the armchair. I do a foolish thing and ask him if he's all right.

'I'll never be all right!' he shouts. 'Don't keep asking me. You're the cause of all this! Don't you understand?'

SATURDAY 6 JUNE 1987

Mal's out valeting cars this morning. I want to talk to Ron but he told me he's taking the rental car back to Isle of Wight today. I'm getting rather anxious about our relationship – it feels as if the longer we are apart the worse it is. I want to be with him for reassurance, not stuck here prolonging the agony. But my hands are tied.

I take Grace to Cambridge to buy her some new school shoes but she's not well – she keeps close to the toilets all afternoon. She's obviously in a lot of distress but she won't open up and tell me how she feels or what's wrong. It seems she can't talk to me about anything anymore. After a couple of hours we go home without any shoes. She lies on her bed and doesn't want anything to eat. I have never felt so helpless a mother as I do today.

I had planned to take Grace with me to Mum's tomorrow, hoping it would restore some normality, but it doesn't look likely now. She stays in her bedroom all evening with the door closed. Mal goes to work and I'm grateful for the space. I try to ignore the nagging guilt again, sort out what I'm taking to my new life and start packing.

SUNDAY 7 JUNE 1987

Grace still isn't very well. She lounges about her bedroom all morning but every so often she comes down for another glass of water. She never comes to talk to me or tell me how she is. I've tried but I'm always faced with a shrug. The yawning gap between us is widening daily; I just don't know how to reach her anymore.

I ring Mum and tell her we're not going today. She's disappointed and she's worried about Grace, as am I. She thinks I should take her to the doctor's tomorrow. I give Mum my new address and phone number but somehow it doesn't seem real.

Mal comes home at noon. I take one look at his face and wish I could be with Ron. Grace falls asleep in the afternoon and Mal goes down the pub. I phone Ron but there's no answer. I wonder if he's still on the Isle of Wight enjoying himself then chastise myself for being unfair to him. I decide to finish my packing then Mal comes back.

'You going tomorrow?' he growls.

'Do you want me to?'

'Oh, please your bloody self. It's just...as you were packing... I thought you were. You might as well.'

'OK. Look, I'll go on Tuesday. This is difficult for all of us, you know?'

MONDAY 8 JUNE 1987

While Grace is getting ready for school, I ask her if she wants me to take her to the doctor's but she says it's only her period.

Why couldn't she tell me? I've worried for two days.

'Are you OK?'

She nods.

'You sure?'

Another nod. 'You don't have to worry about me.' She slings her bag over her shoulder, runs downstairs and out the front door.

TUESDAY 9 JUNE 1987

I haven't slept for thinking about today. Mal and Grace are still in bed when I come down, showered and dressed. The sky is wall-to-wall grey. I start to load the Nova, but with alarm I realize I can't fit everything in.

Oh God, I don't want to have to come back.

I try to eat my breakfast but my stomach churns as the sky darkens and the rain lashes the windows. I don't feel like a person embarking on a new and happy life. It wasn't supposed to be like this.

Saying goodbye to Grace is remarkably easy; there are no tears. She nods when I tell her I'll phone her every day at 4o'clock, and goes to get ready for school.

Then it's Mal's turn. We stand awkwardly in the hall like two gun-slingers not knowing which of us will make the first move.

'What a waste of sixteen years,' he whimpers.

'You mustn't think of it like that. Think of the good times.'

'I'm not that strong.'

'Yes, you are. You've got to be, for Grace.'

'Everywhere I look, I see you.'

I hate seeing him in this state; I just want to be out of here. It's getting darker by the minute, the rain is bouncing off the car roof, thunder in the distance. I grab my handbag and run out the door, struggle with the final pieces of luggage, get wet and get in. I turn the key but the engine won't start. I try again. Nothing. 'Bloody shitting hell!' I scream. 'Why today? Come on, you son-of-a-bitch!'

In the rear view mirror I watch Mal close the front door – I can only imagine what's going on in there. I want to be gone. I try turning the key again. And again, with my foot to the floor. The engine suddenly roars into life.

Thank you, God.

But it's raining so hard the wipers can't clear it, even at full pelt. I wipe the condensation off the windscreen and roar up the road without a backward glance, tears of relief pricking my eyes.

I've done it.

It's an exhausting journey – the weather is against me, raining heavily all the way to Petersfield when there is a glimmer of light in the sky.

At 12:15 I pull onto the drive and half expect Ron to come out and greet me but I open the front door to silence. Dark scary doubts crawl into my mind. I walk into the kitchen then go upstairs. With a sinking feeling I realise he's not there. The clouds of guilt are replaced by emptiness and hurt. I walk down to Lottie and Jack's bungalow. They welcome me with smiling faces and a cup of tea.

'Ron's taken the car back this morning owing to the fact that he had an interview at Orpington yesterday,' says Lottie. 'Are you alright, love?'

I nod.

Why didn't he tell me?

'How was the journey?'

'Awful, raining all the way.' I give her a weak smile and take a sip of tea.

'Yes, not much like June, is it?'

Where is he?

We make small talk and I sense they are trying to reassure me. But I can't help feeling abandoned.

Fifteen minutes later Ron strolls in. I smile at him. He smiles half-heartedly and looks away, picks up the newspaper. I get up and kiss him but it's not returned. We walk back to the house with a gulf between us. Fresh twinges of anxiety start to grip me as he tells me about the unsuccessful job interviews he's had. Where's the positive Ron I knew, the happy smile, the optimism?

'I expected to have a job by the time you came back. Nothing has come of all the CVs I've sent out.' He says. 'And most people have told me, at forty, I'm too old to get a job as a rep in the music industry in this country. I've missed the boat. If I'd stayed in England I would be up there with all the managing directors by now.'

If only he hadn't gone to Australia. If only we'd kept in touch. If only...

'I've got another interview in London on Thursday but it doesn't look too promising.'

'Oh dear, I'm sure something will turn up.'

He doesn't answer. He seems a different person. We come in and he chucks the keys on the hall table. I feel my eyebrows shoot up when he tells me he's phoned Claudette.

'Her aunt died on Wednesday. Poor bitch.' He shoots me a look. 'She's gone through hell this week.'

He's angry. Am I supposed to feel sorry for her? I feel a stab of resentment at his concern. He hasn't even asked me about my departure.

Sally comes round with the boys in the evening. I don't want them here. I'm feeling unsettled and unhappy and I don't want them to know.

She sits down. The boys run upstairs to play in the spare room. Sally looks at Ron, then at me. 'How did your departure go?'

Ron goes to the kitchen. I hear him fill the kettle.

'A bit traumatic.'

She sympathizes, 'I can imagine. How did Grace take it?'

'She's OK. I said I'd ring her every day when she comes in from school.'

I know she means well but I don't want to talk about it anymore. Ron comes back with three mugs of steaming tea. He sits at the other end of the room with his, staring at the television. Sally smiles self-consciously and picks up her mug. I'm wishing her drink was cooler so she doesn't have to stay so long. I offer her a biscuit but she declines saying she's just had her dinner.

'How's your business?' I hear myself say. A stupid question when I already know the answer.

She takes another sip of tea and nods. 'It's good, thanks.'

We sit in silence. I search for something else to say but the spontaneity has elapsed. Ron makes no attempt to come to my rescue. He continues watching the television as if there's no one else here.

Finally, Sally leaves her half-drunk cup of tea on the side, collects the boys and says she'll see us later. Ron says a half-hearted goodbye and remains in the same position.

Why?

When Ron and I go to bed, there is no kiss, no caress. He just turns over and goes to sleep. I feel almost as empty as when I lost my dad.

THURSDAY 11 JUNE 1987

I get up early and cook Ron some breakfast before he goes to London. He keeps checking his appearance in the mirror, but I get the impression the ill-fitting light-grey suit has been languishing in the back of the wardrobe for years. His black lace-up shoes, which I've never seen before, are freshly polished. He looks all wrong; I'm used to seeing him in jeans and a sweatshirt.

I run him to the station at nine. He says he'll be back about eight. I welcome the day to myself.

It's the first time I've been on my own in Petersfield. The town is looking pleased with itself in the sunshine. I park the car and breathe in the liberating air, feeling freer than I have for ages, and realise how much I've been overshadowed by Ron's presence. I get the shopping with his likes and dislikes in my ear. I'm tempted to buy some broccoli – *'No, not that!* *'Her indoors' buys that.'* This is how he refers to Claudette. The TV series *Minder* is very popular in Australia and I wonder again what their relationship was like. I'm tempted to sit in the sunny square and order a coffee but a voice is telling me to get back and finish the chores – I want to please Ron when he comes in, show him I'm in control; show him I care.

Back home, I make myself a sandwich and a cup of tea and sit in the sun-drenched garden, the washing gently flapping on the line. A picture of normal domesticity. I feel independent and in control. This is a moment of calm in the middle of a whirlpool of uncertainty. In my mind, I start to redesign the garden. There's not much to it at the moment, just a lawn and flower beds round the edge with a few straggly roses clinging to the fence.

But all too soon my peace is shattered. I hear the front door. Ron comes waltzing in through the garden, looking for me, and I feel curiously resentful.

I jump to attention, not wanting him to think I'm being lazy. 'Hello, I thought you said you'd be home at eight?'

'Yeah, I know.' He smiles like a naughty little boy who's been playing truant. 'I got you something.' He produces an album of theme tunes including the sound track from *The Trap*. He knows I love that film and the music from it and have been searching for it for years. He's hunted the shops and tracked down a copy. I give him a big kiss and a hug, but he seems preoccupied. He looks at the sleeve of the LP and notices the composer's name: Ron Goodwin.

He smiles. 'That's a funny thing; that's Claudette's surname. It's as if I'm married to her and taken her name!'

How can he be so insensitive?

I can't ask if he still has feelings for her. Instead, I change the subject and ask how he got on today.

He tightens his lips to a thin line, takes a breath. 'The man I went to see was an agent called Henry Pratt. I'm reasonably happy with the way it went. I just hope something comes of it.'

'Where was that?'

He doesn't answer straight away. I get the impression he *has* played truant.

'Tottenham Court Road,' he says, as if he's plucked the name of the air.

I ring Grace a bit later than usual, but she's coping well. I see a little light at the end of that particular tunnel.

'What have you been doing today?' she asks.

'Oh, went into Petersfield to get acquainted with the town, did some washing, sat in the little garden.'

'Oh. Nothing *different* then?'

Huh, out of the mouths of babes...

In the evening I try to please Ron by cooking him one of my special chicken curries. I watch him eating it greedily.

'This is good.'

I smile at the compliment. 'I remember a little restaurant in London, called La Barcia.'

He swallows, puts his knife and fork down. Looks up. 'I don't remember that. Where was it?'

'I dunno, but I know we had chicken curry.'

There's a glimmer. He waves his knife. 'Oh, yeah. I know. Near Earl's Court?'

'Mm. You said something like – some people eat to live, but I live to eat.'

'Huh, yeah. Sounds about right!'

We finish our meal and Ron says he wants to take me to the oldest pub in Hampshire, the Red Lion at Chalton.

The lovely thirteenth century pub with stone floors worn to a shine by centuries of feet, is very warm and very busy so we take our drinks out to the sun-bleached porch and sit on the ancient wooden bench. Ron drinks quietly and I'm lost in my own thoughts. I look out towards the dark that seems to be all-encompassing, depressing. I don't want to broach the subject of Ron's job-hunting and I don't want to talk about setting up my hairdressing business until I'm settled.

Ron downs his lager and suggests we go to The Sun at Buriton. More memories. This is Ron's old local that he and Lofty used to frequent. He recognises some people he hasn't seen for years and leaves me sitting on my own to go and talk to them. He looks relaxed and happy but only glances in my direction now and again. He doesn't introduce me or ask me to join them and I feel as uncomfortable sitting here as I did in 1966, my mind working overtime.

When we go to bed, Ron makes a clumsy attempt at sex; he's had too much to drink, rolls over and goes to sleep. He hasn't once told me he loves me since I've been back. I start to make comparisons between Ron and Mal; they're alike in some ways. I get the feeling they would hit it off under different circumstances. And then there are those phone numbers. Am I getting into the same dance with a different partner? I stay awake most of the night while Ron snores.

FRIDAY 12 JUNE 1987

We get up and have a serious talk, the first we've had since I came back on Tuesday. I swallow down the lump in my throat – it doesn't look hopeful that things will work out. After all the reminiscing we've done, Ron asks if I'm in love with a memory. I can't answer him. I refuse to believe it. I'm not only in love with the Ron I knew twenty years ago.

We go to Portsmouth to see Madge at her printing works and Ron picks up his CVs she's typed for him. Finding work takes priority in his life now and he pushes me aside, like a toy of which he's grown tired. Madge asks how I am. I put on a brave face and say I'm fine – I don't want anyone to know the illusion has been shattered.

Ron suggests a walk on Butser Hill in the afternoon. I park the car and we stand in the green wide-open space. I fill my lungs with the clear air and take in the beautiful patchwork fields in the distance but a heavy grey mist is rolling in, clouding my view. We both pretend there is nothing wrong and take photos of each other, trying to enjoy the afternoon. But I have to keep pressing down the tears lurking under the surface. I turn into the wind, a romantic sorrow stirring my soul.

'I want that God should see me in the face.'

I'm lost in my thoughts. Does God know how I feel at this moment? Why was this meant to happen if not to bring us together? I can't believe it's all been for nothing. Is Fate putting me through a transition and using Ron as the medium? If so, is he aware?

Ron brings me back to the present, says he'll cook dinner tonight. I welcome it. This is something Mal never did. I find myself making comparisons all the time, looking for signposts.

Back at the house, he starts to prepare a bolognese. But first, he pours a gin and tonic for me and a Foster's for himself. In no time he's opened a second can. Why do I always pick the blokes who like a drink? At the back of my diary I have started to make a list of similarities between Ron and Mal. I list the pros and cons for both. Ron has more positives, which is a good sign, but I can't stop analysing the situation. Ron's oblivious to all this; he's stopped reading my diary long ago.

He shouts from the kitchen, 'The bolognese looks more like a chilli!'

I go in and stare at the pan. 'Ha! We'll have chilli instead, then.'

'I don't know what happened there. Just kept adding things and got a bit carried away!' He giggles, his face aglow.

I love you.

'It doesn't matter. I'm sure it's very tasty.'

I drape my arms round his neck and kiss him. He gives me a childish grin and turns back to the stove, dishes up two platefuls of rich mahogany mush and pasta. We devour it and after a few more drinks Ron suggests we walk into town. He wants to show me two more watering holes – The Oak, which is a bit young for us with lots of loud music pumping out, and The Drum, which we joke is 'Hum-Drum'. We have a couple of drinks in each and come home. More talking, more drinking: a large gin and tonic for me and a bourbon and coke for him.

Ron says, 'I think the best thing that will probably come out of all of this is a good friendship, but give it another week... Things could be different when I get a job.'

SATURDAY 13 JUNE 1987

I get up early and ponder over last night. Should I give it more time or is it hopeless? One half of me wants to hang on to what we had, the other doesn't want to waste time on a platonic relationship. I'm on the point of phoning Mal when Ron gets up. We talk philosophically, trying to find out how we both feel deep down. I have never talked like this with anyone but I'm not entirely sure it helps. All it does, for me, is to make me examine my motives and my character. I'm exposed and uncomfortable.

Ron goes down to see Lottie and Jack, comes back with a newspaper and spreads it out on the kitchen worktop, scanning for jobs, yet again.

'Lottie asked after you. She said, 'I hope she stays.''

'Did she?'

'Yeah. Ooh, scratch me back!'

I endeavour to relieve him of the itch while he leans on the worktop.

'No, bit further down. That's it!'

'Like an old dog! Did you know you were born in the Chinese year of the Dog?'

'Ha. Woof!'

This small window of intimacy over, he turns back to the jobs. 'I said we'd go and watch Richard play football this afternoon – put a smile on the little bugger's face.'

'Sure. I don't know much about football, though.'

'That's OK, you don't have to, just so long as he sees us. It'll be a nice surprise for him.'

I find it very difficult to stay positive as I drive to the football club. I park in the muddy field, the grey sky heavy with rain. The cold rises up and strikes into my bones and into my heart. We pick our way through the mud towards the refreshment tent.

I ask Ron if he'd like a nice hot cup of tea then find myself asking him if he wants milk and one sugar. Why did I do that? I know perfectly well how he likes it. I take the hot tea in paper cups that scorch my fingers, and lurch over the bumpy ground to where Ron and Martin are standing. Ron takes his without acknowledgement, feigning interest in the game. Martin asks if I've done anything more about setting up my hairdressing business. I have to confess I haven't, but I can't tell him why. I sense Martin's disapproval keenly but he says nothing. Ron, Martin and I all stand apart like three strangers. And Richard hasn't noticed we've come to watch him play.

We drive back in silence.

Ron volunteers to cook steak for dinner the way they do in Australia – heating the non-stick frying pan first without any oil, so it gets really hot. He's enjoying showing off his skills. He's always talking about how things are done in Australia and how positive it is but this only serves to strike fear into my heart. He holds his hand over the pan to test for temperature, taking care not to touch it, then throws in the steaks. They sizzle and smell divine. He's already cooked the chips and vegetables. As I watch him taking care over it I pray to God a job comes up soon. The meal is good, as I knew it would be, accompanied by a bottle of Roussillon.

Afterwards, we walk to a wine bar in Petersfield. Ron orders a bottle of Rosemount chardonnay and starts a conversation with the barman about Australian wines. Ron picks up his glass, takes a mouthful and urges the barman and me to do the same.

'What d'you think?'

The barman nods. 'Yeah, I've tasted it before. It's good. It's becoming very popular with our customers.'

Ron beams.

I take a sip. It's very strong-tasting wine aged in oak barrels. When the barman is called away behind the bar, Ron tells me he's very disillusioned with England – too much apathy.

'I'm gonna give it six months, then if it doesn't come together I'm going back to Australia.' He drains his glass to emphasise the point.

My heart sinks.

We go home and have another couple of drinks and listen to some music. Then suddenly Ron says, 'Let's go to bed and be nice to each other.'

I follow him upstairs and watch him get undressed. I do the same, hoping that this time it will happen naturally. But he's rough with me – there's no preparation, no gentleness. It leaves me cold. He turns over and goes to sleep. I'm left staring at the ceiling, feeling too baffled by his behaviour to cry.

SUNDAY 14 JUNE 1987

I get up and have another think. Perhaps if we'd had a courting period? We've both come straight out of one frying pan into another. There hasn't been enough time to let things develop.

I need to phone Mum today, too, but I don't know quite what to say – I don't want to worry her, but I feel I should go and see her for a couple of days, maybe longer. It crosses my mind that maybe I should look for a flat in the Margate area to be near her. I feel very unsettled, negative. I mention to Ron that I want to phone her but I'm not sure how to start, what to say.

'How about, 'how are you'? That's always a good way to start.'

Yes, of course. Ron is a good person with empathy for others. He makes it all sound so easy. He said one day at the beginning, 'We're learning from each other, aren't we?' I hope this is still true. Yes, of course, how are you. The rest should be easy after that. I pick up the phone.

'Hello, Mum. How are you?'

'Oh, all right. What about you?'

'I'm fine. I'm coming down for a couple of days on Tuesday, if that's OK?'

'Yes, all right. I'm going into hospital again tomorrow for some more treatment, but I should be all right by then. Herbie wants a word,' she passes the phone to him.

'Hello, Julie. Everything all right?'

'I think so. How are you?'

'I'm getting engaged to Bridget! What do you think to that?'

My heart leaps for him. 'Oh, that's wonderful! I'm really pleased for you.'

They met about two months ago, but I've been too wrapped up my own life to notice how much they meant to each other. It's a fairy tale romance but I can't see my story having a happy ending.

I tell Herbie I'll be down on Tuesday and look forward to celebrating with him. But I'm worried that Mum is having more treatment. I will have to look into this.

It's another day – another reason to be hopeful that Ron and I will turn a corner. The sun is shining, a good omen. Ron takes me to The Harrow at lunchtime. We take our drinks outside and sit in the pub garden.

'Herbie's getting engaged,' I tell him.

Ron beams. 'Wow, fantastic! That's great news.'

We drink to Herbie and Bridget, lifting our glasses high in the air. He's genuinely happy for them, even though he's never met them.

We go to Lottie and Jack's for Sunday lunch and open the door onto the appetising aroma of roast lamb. Ron's favourite of course. It's obvious Lottie is doing all she can to please her son. Roast lamb was always my favourite, too. Lottie would be such a good mother-in-law; I so want to be part of this big happy family but feel the chance is slipping further and further away.

Ron suggests we go to Buriton in the afternoon, his old home. I park the car and we walk around the deserted village. He walks on ahead of me. I take photos, trying to take comfort from the sun glinting through the trees, but there's no denying the despair and the sadness bubbling away inside me. We come upon a cricket match on the green and we watch for a while.

Ron takes my hand, still focused on the scene. 'Mm, very English.'

Apart from these few words he's very distant. I pray to God he gets the job he's going after on Wednesday. Maybe, just maybe, things will improve. But right now it's as if I don't exist.

We come back to the house and Ron switches on the television. It's an old Western but I can't concentrate on it. My eyelids are heavy with sleep deprivation, but I can't give in to it knowing how Ron feels. I force myself to stay awake and ask when he wants me to cut his hair.

He stares at me. 'That's incredible. You won't believe this, but I was just thinking about you cutting my hair!'

'I can believe it. It's only people who are spiritually close can communicate like that.'

He shakes his head and sighs, gives me a searching look.

I smile. 'We're still learning from each other...'

It's difficult to read his expression. For a few seconds, time stands still then he turns back to the screen.

In the evening, Ron suggests we take the rest of the chilli and a bottle of wine across the road to Alison and Robert– they're a young couple with two young children who don't get out much. I'm happy to go along with this to make new friends. Ron takes a video of the Australian outback to show them, but he puts it on and sits glued to it. I feel very awkward with his back to me but I try to make conversation with Alison. She's a young mum without the help of family in the area and I start to compare hers with my own situation when Grace was little. But I can't talk about that; it feels disloyal. I can only nod in all the right places. Ron isn't interested in anything but the video. He gets stuck into the wine and ignores us.

When I go up to the bathroom I come out to I find a little girl in her nightie, standing barefoot on the landing, looking bewildered.

'Hello. Who are you?'

No reply.

'Have you had a bad dream?'

Nothing.

'Do you want your mummy?'

She nods.

'Come on, then. Come downstairs with me.' I take the child's bed-warm hand and lead her downstairs. Images of Grace at the same age flood my mind, and my heart goes out to them both.

'Look who I've found!' I say to no one in particular. 'She was standing on the landing.'

Ron looks up very briefly but makes no remark. This isn't like him, he usually loves children. Alison takes charge and her little daughter is soon tucked back up in bed. They're a nice couple, Alison and Robert, and when Ron finally drags himself away from the screen, we have a nice evening. It makes a refreshing change to be in the company of another couple and I hope Alison and I will become friends.

We come home and go to bed. This time Ron's more attentive; his kisses are passionate, he encourages me to fold myself around him and I know, given time, we could be so good together. Our bodies fit so well. But all of a sudden he says, 'Mustn't let him come in there! That *would* be silly.'

This pours cold water on my desire. We have never discussed birth control; it has never come up in conversation and I haven't had to worry about it for years — sex with Mal was rare. I have never been able to take the pill because of my medical history and we had our own way of handling contraception.

Ron is asleep before I can begin to voice my thoughts on the subject and I start to wonder again if I should stay. I decide to see what happens tomorrow.

MONDAY 15 JUNE 1987

I get up and go to the bathroom. Oh, no! Another period. It's only seventeen days since the last one.

There must be something wrong with me.

Fate is having a ball; I imagine the Gods laughing at me. I also know I've lost weight. When I step on the scales they confirm this – nine stone – I'm usually nine stone ten. I examine myself in the mirror. Spots on my bony chest, I feel a wreck.

What's happening to me?

I run downstairs and mention my weight loss to Ron. He looks up briefly from the literature spread out on the table, shakes his head. 'That's no good. I like meat on my women. Your hair needs to be longer, too.'

This tactless remark chips another piece off my confidence, but I bury it. He's busy organising his day, oblivious to anything else.

'I want to go to Chichester to check out Marine Security Systems, the place where I'm having the interview on Wednesday. It'll be a good idea to pick up some literature on the things I'll be selling, *if* I get the job.' A half smile. I wish he'd smile more; it makes my heart sing.

It's the first time I've been to Chichester, it's a lovely old town. But as we stroll along in the sunshine he barely holds my hand, and when I take hold of his it's like a piece of unyielding leather.

We find the chandlery. Ron goes up to the desk, introduces himself to the receptionist and tells her he's got an interview on Wednesday. She's very impressed he's taken the trouble to find out about the company.

He looks round at me as if to say, See? This is how it's done.

I hope it puts him in good stead. He's now down to his last few pounds. As we leave, I feel very awkward about his situation and ask if he has any regrets.

'Nah,' he insists, 'You should never waste time on regrets; you should only learn from your experiences and move on.'

He speaks with such conviction – if he truly believes this, what a wonderful philosophical outlook.

'Come on. I'll take you to Bosham where King Canute's daughter is buried. You'll like it there.'

He's right. It's a magical place right on the shoreline. Ron says the causeway floods at high tide and cuts you off if you're not aware of it. Fortunately there are two ways to reach the church and as we walk through the little village he tells me King Canute had a house here and later, King Harold inherited the manor from his father, Godwin. The little church dates back to Saxon times and is depicted in the Bayeux Tapestry. The Latin apparently tells us 'Harold, Earl of the English and his Knights ride to Bosham'.

The old oak door creaks open to the smell of old timbers, opening up a world of history stretching back centuries. The Saxon tower is the oldest part. No doubt about it, Ron knows some beautiful places. But I can hardly take in all he's telling me. Thinking about our relationship and wondering how much time I have left with him is clouding everything. We walk around separately investigating the surroundings but try as I might, I can't remain upbeat and positive.

I'm losing him.

Next he directs me to a beautiful little harbour inlet. The sun is glinting on the water like thousands of diamonds on blue silk. Chalk-white clouds in the ultramarine sky.

We find ourselves walking up the steps to a marine bar overlooking the boats and dinghies bobbing gently in the water. The place is empty save for the barman. Ron doesn't want anything to eat but I'm starving, which is unusual. I order a smoked mackerel salad and sit at the polished oak bar on my own, taking in the beauty of the harbour scene through the open window. Ron sits on his own at one of the tables with a pint of Foster's and starts in earnest pawing over the literature from Marine Security Systems.

I'm enjoying the peace and tranquillity when Ron says we have to go in to Portsmouth to buy yet more shopping. He also has an appointment to see Robert at four-thirty about a business proposition.

Outside Robert's business premises on the industrial estate, I ring Grace from a call box while Ron waits outside.

Grace sounds miserable. 'Dad's down to his last eighteen pounds in the bank after paying for a load of your stuff.'

I suppress my temper. 'What stuff? I don't owe any money.'

'I don't know, but he's not very happy.'

I blow out a sigh. 'OK. I'll be at Nanna's tomorrow if he wants to phone me there.'

'All right, I'll tell him.'

'Are you OK? Are you coping?'

'Yeah, I s'pose...'

'Listen, I'll phone you tomorrow. From Nanna's. OK?'

She grunts. I step out of the phone box and look down at my feet, then up to heaven. 'Oh God, I'm worried, I don't know what Grace is talking about. She says I owe Mal a lot of money.'

Ron moves closer. 'You should phone him tonight from a call box, that way you can say what you want.'

What does he think I want to say?

Ron goes to see Robert earlier than planned while I sit in the car staring at the now grey sky, wishing everything was resolved. Should I go? Should I stay? How does Ron really feel about me now? How do I feel about him? Is it worth pursuing? And added to all this is the money I'm supposed to owe Mal. Anger bubbles up in my chest. Is that *all* he's worried about when it boils down to it? The money?

After about ten minutes Ron comes back and sits beside me.

'I stood and watched you there for a minute. Got a lot on your mind, haven't you?' He takes a breath and shouts. 'Christ! You looked so bloody *miserable.*'

It's like a dagger through my heart. I want to cry. There's no point continuing with this. It's finished. There's no reason for me to come back at the weekend either.

We come back and I run upstairs, craving space. I still don't have it even after stressing my need. I start packing, again. I look at the single unmade bed in the spare room and wonder if it might have made any difference if we'd slept separately at the beginning. More time to get our feelings in order?

Ron rushes upstairs and makes me jump; he's looking for something. 'I'm losing my flatmate,' he says, his back turned to me.

I want him to say, 'Please stay,' to put his arms round me, to comfort me, stop me from leaving. But he finds what he was looking for and goes back downstairs without another word.

I go out to ring Mal, but as I walk I'm in two minds – should I or shouldn't I? It's going to be awkward. What do I say? Without any warning the clouds open and big raindrops splash on the pavement then couple up. Within seconds it turns into sheet rain and

I run for cover, wrench open the door of the call box and wipe my hands down my jeans. I dial the number. But it just rings and rings. I step out to bright sunshine – the rain has stopped as abruptly as it started. Had I waited, maybe Ron would've tried to stop me, told me to stay. Fate is playing a devilish game with me and I'm failing to read the signs.

I come back and tell Ron I'll pay for a meal in the Beefeater tonight, as it's our last night together.

His face lights up. 'Thank you. I'll return it when I get a job.'

I shake my head, 'you don't have to. I *want* to do it.'

'You know, when your back's against the wall and your arse is on the floor, the only way is up and forward.'

This isn't the first time he's said this. I wonder if he truly believes it. It's almost as if someone else is whispering in his ear.

The Beefeater is warm and welcoming as usual. We order our steaks and a bottle of Côte du Rhone and sit down to our last supper.

The wine loosens Ron's tension. 'For a little woman, you're good on the fang!' he says again.

I smile, the first time for ages.

'I think, when we meet up next time, things could be different. But at the moment, what's come out of this is a very strong friendship.'

I wonder if there'll be a next time; only time will tell. But for now, I feel there's a lot more than friendship, more of a spiritual bond. I've never been in this strange situation before and I'm finding it incredible. Most of the time I instinctively know what he's thinking, and I feel it's the same for him with me. But it's more than telepathy. It's as if our two spirits are connected.

We go to The Good Intent afterwards for a couple more drinks. He seems *intent* on sinking as much beer as possible but I can't say anything. It's good to see him happy.

Back at the house Ron pours more drinks and I decide to play a game with him. I put on one of my dad's old LPs that I've brought with me – a jazz pianist from way back – and ask him who he thinks it is. He looks thoughtful.

'Hmm, I don't know. Hang on, don't tell me.' He taps his forehead.

I just wish our relationship could run full circle. Just one more hurdle...

'I was going to say Dudley Moore, but it's too sophisticated for him.' He listens a while longer. Takes two more gulps of his drink.

'Give in?'

'Yeah, I'm afraid you've got me this time.'

'It's Errol Garner! *Errol's Bounce.*'

'Oh, yeah, he's great! I'd forgotten all about him.'

We finish listening to the track then Ron starts rummaging through some of his boxes. He produces a record. 'Here,' he says, 'let's see what you make of this.'

It sounds familiar but I'm not sure who it is. Ron smiles; he's got his own back. He drains his drink and pours another, sits smiling at me, waiting for an answer.

I love you.

'Well?'

I shake my head. 'No. You've won!'

'Ha! Gino Washington and the Ram Jam Band!'

'Of course! They used to play at The Black Prince on Sundays – R and B night!'

'Yeah, they would've played at clubs like that. This is live.'

'God! That takes me back.' I reminisce about the old days when Lorn and I used to dance the night away together. Happy times. Ron of course, has never met her but I often mention her rune readings. I need to see Lorn; she'd be interested in what's going on at the moment and no doubt have some advice for me. The rune reading she gave me all those months ago, when she came to stay, was very accurate. I have studied it recently. If only I had heeded their advice I might not be drifting without a paddle right now. Everything would've worked out, maybe.

Ron shakes me out of my reverie.

'Drink up! I'll get us another.' Ron pours two more gin and tonics and we talk some more about the old days. I remember him coming out of The Black Prince one evening and walking past a brand new red Sunbeam Alpine.

'Do you remember what you said?'

'Nope, go on.'

'You said, Get away with that Alpine before I jump on it!'

He frowns. 'Did I? I don't remember saying that.'

I nod. 'Well, you did.'

'How come you remember all this stuff?'

How indeed.

We drink and dance to the music until I fall onto his lap and drape my arms round his neck. I sink into him, getting close to his spirit. Snuggle into his warmth and kiss him. 'You're a wonderful person and I love you very, very much.'

He takes another slurp of his drink and slurs, 'So are you, and I love you very much, too.' Then he lightens the mood, grins through his stupor. 'If nothing else, we're good drinking partners!'

TUESDAY 16 JUNE 1987

I wake early, very confused after last night. We had such a good time that I'm wondering if I should come back at the weekend. Should I even be leaving today? Ron is still unconscious when I get up. I finish packing and have a shower.

While I start to pack the car, Ron cooks a lovely breakfast of fried bacon, eggs, tomatoes and mushrooms and tells me it'll set me up for the long journey. I feel cared for and mourn the fact that I'm leaving him. He keeps saying: 'It hasn't worked out this time round, but who knows what'll happen in the future?' Maybe we're both grabbing at straws. While I'm getting ready, Ron plays the theme from *The Trap*.

'Every time you hear this you'll think of me,' he says conceitedly.

But I know it's true. While I listen I brace myself for breaking the news to Lottie and Jack. This wasn't supposed to happen – we were supposed to be the golden couple living in harmony for the rest of our lives.

My heavy sadness makes it difficult to drag my feet along to Lottie and Jack's. I take a deep breath and knock on their door.

'Hello, love,' says Lottie, welcoming as always. 'Come in.'

Her brightness masks the underlying tension but I'm sure she knows what's coming. I follow her into the living room and she looks up at me expectantly. I swallow hard, my heart thumping. 'I've come to say goodbye. It's not going to work out.'

She has compassion written all over her face, 'Never mind, love. I had a feeling it wouldn't; it's been a long time and people change. Better you found out now than later.'

She gives me a hug and my eyes fill. 'I'm so sorry, I so wanted it to.'

'I know you did, love. So did Ron. We all did.' She's thinking what else to say, then, 'I don't suppose you're compatible; Jack and I weren't compatible when we first got married.'

I don't want to argue. 'Where is Jack?'

'He's popped into town for some batteries for his razor. He shouldn't be long. Shall I put the kettle on?'

'Oh, no thanks, Lottie. I don't think I'll have time.' I look at my watch and wonder how long I'll have to wait for Jack. Lottie goes back to the kitchen and I perch on the edge of her floral patterned sofa. Now that I've told her I'm going, I want to be away. I feel out of place. And I don't want to go through all this again with Jack. I go to the kitchen and find Lottie peeling potatoes at the sink.

'I'm sorry, Lottie, but I should be on my way.'

She stops peeling the potatoes and dries her hands on her pinny. 'All right, love. Keep in touch, won't you?'

I nod. 'I will.'

She follows me to the front door. There's so much I want to say to her but the words refuse to form themselves. I stand bravely waiting for my mother-in-law-who-never-was to say her last few words.

She clasps my hands in hers. 'Goodbye, love. Have a safe journey. And don't forget – come and see us again.'

I nod and kiss her soft cheek. Step over the threshold into the unknown. Like a helium-filled balloon about to be released into the atmosphere, I have no idea where I'll end up. I can only focus on the immediate future – the journey to Mum's and the familiarity of home. Then there's Grace. And Mal. How am I going to face them after all the upset I've caused? I'm dreading their reaction.

I find myself putting my belongings in the car. Ron has disappeared. I carry the last of my bags to the boot and slam it then he comes downstairs. He ignores me and starts tidying the living room, plumping up cushions, clearing me away. This episode of his life is already closed.

I stand awkwardly in the middle of the floor and wait. But he says nothing.

'Well,' I swallow, 'I think I've got everything.'

'Yeah, O.K.,' he says, matter-of-factly, as if I'm going on a short break. 'If you've forgotten anything I'll post it on to you.'

'Thanks.'

After all we've been through and all we are to each other, is this all?

He follows me out to the car. This feels all wrong; I feel empty and sad as if there's something missing. I turn to face him. 'Thanks for everything. I'll keep in touch.'

'No problem. I'll keep in touch, too. Have a good journey. No wrong turns!'

I smile and give him a kiss, but it's not reciprocated. I search his face for a message, but I can't read it. It's no good; I need to tell him how I feel. 'You're a wonderful person. Remember – I'll always keep you in a special corner of my heart.' I have never put so much feeling into a single sentence.

'Yeah, me too. Look after yourself.'

I've been signed off. The unspoken 'it's-been-nice-knowing-you' hangs in the air.

I put the Nova in gear and, unlike my departure from Melbourne, the engine roars into life. Ron, without waving goodbye, goes back inside and closes the door.

My mind races on during the two-and-three-quarter hour journey. This was all meant to happen for a reason. A powerful energy has snatched me out of my old life and dropped me into the new. The fulfilling of our relationship wasn't meant to happen twenty years ago, and it's not meant to happen now. Ron was just the instrument, the means by which to set me on a new course. My higher self has kicked in and I firmly believe this. Maybe, in time, I will get back with Mal, but not yet. I need some breathing space, to live on my own for a while, to grow and develop spiritually. Then I will be ready to come to the right decision. But this isn't only about me. There's poor Grace. It'll need more than a hug and a kiss to heal those gaping wounds.

I reach Margate feeling strangely exhilarated. I tell Mum that nothing has come of my stay with Ron except a very strong friendship. She looks confused. Hardly surprising.

'What about Mal? Don't you want to go back to him?'

'No, Mum. I don't know where I want to be at the moment. I think I need some time on my own. I expect something will turn up.'

Her brow furrows, 'Oh, dear. I hope you'll be all right.'

I kiss her on the cheek. 'I'll be fine.'

I ring Ron.

'Hello. How's my little Vegemite? Journey OK?'

'Yeah, fine. No wrong turns. I did a lot of thinking on the way and came up with some answers.'

'Oh, good, I'm glad one of us has!'

'Yeah. Thank you for being there when I needed you; it couldn't have happened with a nicer person.'

'Thank you. I feel the same.'

'Good luck with the interview tomorrow.'

'Thanks. I'll keep in touch and let you know what happens; I'm pretty confident.'

'Good, that's what I like to hear. Speak to you soon.'

I relax in Mum's little garden with the view across fields of cabbages, the sun beating down. I've only been separated from Ron for a few hours but already I feel lost. I have failed. How am I going to face everyone? What will Mal say? I've put him through hell to be with Ron. Now I'm back, like a naughty child who pestered for a new toy only to realise it wasn't what they wanted.

I pluck up the courage and ring Mal in the evening. 'How are you?'

'Huh, still floating around without an anchor,' he moans.

'Grace said I owe you a lot of money. What's that all about?' I sound like a school teacher.

'It's nothing to do with you; she got it all wrong. I'll work it out.'

'Oh, good. I've been a bit worried.' I pause and brace myself. Here goes. 'I need to talk to you.'

I can feel the tension coming down the phone. 'What about?'

'Well, I'm at Mum's. I don't know where I'm going at the moment.'

'What?' he spits. 'What's wrong? What do you want?'

'I want to live on my own; I want to talk to you about it.'

He heaves a long drawn-out sigh. I have a mental picture of him rubbing a hand over his face. 'I'll always be here when you need me, you know that.'

'Well, I think I need you now.'

I can hear the fear in his voice. 'What is it? You sound as if you want to run away from something.'

I take a deep breath. 'How do you feel about me living on my own, maybe see you now and again and maybe start from scratch?'

'Aw,' he breaths, 'I'd love that! I'll be down tonight to discuss it. Be about nine-thirty OK?'

'Yeah. Thanks.' I don't feel as excited as Mal. In fact, I feel I'm giving him false hope and betraying Ron. No sooner have I put the phone down, it rings again.

'You've left your camera behind!' Giggles Ron.

'Yeah, I realised that halfway up the A272.'

'Let me know where you are and I'll post it on to you.'

'Thanks... I've just phoned Mal. He's coming down tonight. He's going to help me find somewhere to live.'

'Oh, good. You sound very chirpy.'

'Do I?'

'Yeah. Anyhow, let me know how you get on.'

Why have I left my camera behind? Is it my bit of insurance, a subconscious reason to go back?

Mal comes down dead on nine-thirty. He looks awkward standing on the front step, hopping from one foot to the other. He stays outside while I get my jacket. We walk to the Wheatsheaf so we can talk without Mum or anyone listening in. After a couple of drinks I feel less awkward and start to open up to him. I express my need to live up in the Royston area so I can be near Grace. He's fine with that.

'You've got a letter at home. I'm sorry, but I opened it. One of your customers has written offering the use of her caravan as a bolthole, *if* you need it.'

This sounds like Marjorie at Windy Ridge Kennels, another of my customers and a friend of Pauline's – news has travelled.

'Come up at the weekend,' says Mal, 'I'm away and Grace is going to Mum's. You'll have the place to yourself; your own space.' He suddenly smiles, shyly. 'I've already bought your gin and tonic!'

I'm playing right into his hands, I can feel it. I sit opposite Mal, something that Ron's taught me, but he seems like a stranger when I look into his pale blue eyes. I don't feel any love for him. I can't picture getting back with him. I wish with all my heart that Ron was sitting opposite me instead.

We walk back to Mum's with a yawning gulf between us. I feel completely disengaged from Mal now, as if I left him years ago. We say goodbye at the door and I thank him for coming.

WEDNESDAY 17 JUNE 1987

I wake with a jolt. *What the hell am I doing? I can't accept Ron will never to be part of my future. Why has it all gone wrong? Why hasn't sex been fulfilling? None of it makes any sense.*

I'm on my own; everyone else has gone to work. I get up and stir myself into action, make a cup of tea and try to organize my day.

I can hear Ron telling me what to do, 'Be positive. Sort yourself out. Get your head together. Don't think about it, do it!'

I ring Marjorie at the kennels. She's terribly sorry to hear that things haven't worked out and offers me the use of her caravan in her garden.

'I won't gloss it over, Julie – it's a bit dilapidated – but right now it's any port in a storm, isn't it?'

'Thanks, Marjorie. Can I come and see you on Saturday? I'll be up in Melbourn for the weekend.'

'Of course, I look forward to it.'

I feel a bit happier now; I have friends at least. I put down the phone and wonder. *Will my living near Mal make things difficult for him. No. It won't work.*

I pick up the phone again and ring Ron. I have to know what went wrong between us.

'Hello,' he says, sleepily. 'How are you?'

'Oh, not bad. I really need to talk to you.'

'Yeah? What about?'

Oh, God. 'Well, I just wondered if you'd thought any more about what went wrong between us? I'm really struggling to come to terms with this.'

A long pause, I hear him sucking in his lips, then a sigh. 'Yeah, I know what you mean. I'm afraid I don't have any answers, mate.'

Not the reaction I was hoping for. Something tells me he's looking for the next adventure, the next project to get his teeth into.

He clears his throat. 'I'm fairly confident of getting this job. The interview went well, yesterday. I'll probably know on Monday.'

'Oh, that's good.'

'Yeah.'

I can feel his uncertainty while he's fishing for words.

'Remember,' he reinforces, 'my inner strength is your inner strength. I wish it could have been different, too. I feel the same as you. Down.'

This is something of a revelation but I play him at his own game, try to sound optimistic. 'OK. I'll speak to you soon. Good luck for Monday.'

When I'm with Mum and Tom at the working men's club in the evening, I give her Ron's letter to read, the encouraging one from Australia with *The Present* and *The Future*. I find it hard to believe he's written it now, but it's a part of him – the part that gave me hope. Gave us both hope.

Mum gives it back to me and smiles broadly. 'Well, with a letter like that, I think you should go back and give it another try...'

'Do you?'

She nods enthusiastically.

I decide to phone Ron tomorrow and see if he agrees. After all, we've both given up a lot to be together.

THURSDAY 18 JUNE 1987

I use the phone on the landing and dial Ron's number but there's no answer. I try and read the signposts but fail. Then, in the afternoon, Ron rings to tell me I have a letter there.

'Keep it for me; I'm coming back on Sunday to give it another try!'

There's a smile in his voice, but only a small one. 'That's good news.'

'I can't leave it like this. I think we need each other.'

'Yeah, I think you're right,' he says, unconvincingly.

I'm not sure of anything anymore.

I ring Grace and tell her what I'm doing. She says she'll tell her dad when he comes home.

Mal rings at 8pm. 'You're a hard woman,' he shouts, so loud I have to hold the phone away from my ear. Mum looks worryingly at me. I gesture to her that it's OK.

'There's no compassion in you anymore. If you go back down there, I never want to see you again. When you want to see Grace you'll have to come when I'm out. You didn't even have the decency to phone me, I had to phone you. Start looking at yourself. I'm not going to be hurt anymore.'

I feel like a child after a good scolding.

'Poor Grace has done all your washing, take all your stuff and go. You keep comparing me with *him,* messing me about. And another thing, take a tip from me and smarten yourself up. This Ron sounds like a *chancer*; if you go with him and things don't work out this time, I'll cut you off and you'll be completely on your own!' He slams down the phone.

I'm thrown off my axis; my conscience thinks he's right. I phone Ron to tell him we should just stay friends, but there's no answer. Fate is still calling the shots.

I go upstairs to be alone and pace the floor in a grey cloud of quandary. After ten minutes I pick up the phone and dial Mal's number.

'I had to be sharp with you to make you see sense,' he says. 'Come up at the weekend, and I'll take Monday and Tuesday off to see if we can find you a place and get you sorted out. I'm still your best friend. We'll work it out, what went wrong...with **us**.'

'I can't bounce straight back to you! I want to live on my own.'

'Why? Why do you want to escape? Is it that you don't want family life?'

Maybe there's an element of truth in this. Grace came along before we had a chance to make a life for ourselves. We were too young.

'I don't know. You probably hate Ron, but I think he's taught me a lot. You might even thank him one day. He said, you must tell each other how you feel, do things together.'

'Sounds like good advice. I'm not going to argue with that.'

I sit on the top stair and mull it over. Eventually I decide to get it all cleared up tonight; it's not fair to leave Ron dangling either. 11pm. I ring his number, knowing he'll still be up.

'I'm sorry, but I'm not coming back on Sunday. I've done a lot of thinking and come to the conclusion that it's best left like this. If it doesn't work out a second time we would ruin a valued friendship. You said yourself, friendship means everything. I've made up my mind and closed all the doors.'

'Well, close my door but keep the window open! Sort yourself out and I wish you all the best for the future. I'll send your camera and your letters on to Melbourn.'

'Thanks. How do you feel?'

'Confused!'

'Oh, I'm sorry.' This hardly seems enough under the circumstances, but I can't think of anything else. Then I remember what Ron would say and get in first. 'Don't forget – keep in touch.'

'Of course.'

I come off the phone and tell Herbie.

'Happy with your decision?'

I nod. 'You know it's right, too, don't you?'

'Yes, you are doing the right thing.'

We hug each other and the closeness of my big little brother fills me up.

FRIDAY 19 JUNE 1987

I mope around the house all day; life feels pointless. I shampoo and set Mum's hair and cut Herbie's and feel a bit more positive after that. Huh, positive. One of Ron's words. There's no getting away from it, his words are part of me now.

I look back over my diary entries at Ron's explanation of what his phone number means. 68792 = six months of turmoil in 87, nine months to sort myself out and by the second month next year, everything will have settled down. 'Perhaps it will be the same for him?' I write, 'I hold him in my fondest memory.'

Mum shouts up the stairs and shakes me back to reality.

'Julie?'

'Yes?'

'Would you like to go out with Tom and me tonight down to the working men's club?'

I take a while to answer. I know they're only trying to help but it's not really my type of place. 'OK,' I shout back half-heartedly.

I know Ron would have wanted me to go, but when I get in there, I feel as if I've left my positive self at the door. Most of the people are over sixty and all have partners. Are they all happy? Is Mum really happy with Tom? He's so different to Dad. He had style with a capital S – his Cark Gable image, his easy manner. Everyone noticed when he walked into a room. God, I miss him.

Mum is talking to her friend Rose whose husband is playing snooker with Tom. I'm the youngest woman in the club. I sit listening to the fifties pop music and country songs, some of which Ron has played in the past. But I feel conspicuous – I hate the leering looks I keep getting from the younger, unattractive men. I am desperately missing Ron and feel like crawling into a corner.

Tom buys Mum and me another drink. I sit staring into mine, wishing I was still in Petersfield. Mum is giving me worried looks but trying to put on a brave face as she chats to Rose. The evening drags. I can't wait to leave. When Mum and Tom say their goodbyes at the door, I hear one of the younger men say to Mum, 'Is that your daughter, Joyce?'

She nods, full of pride but I'm already out the door.

'Is she looking for a partner?' I hear him say.

I have walked on. I hear her call me back but no way am I going to turn round.

SATURDAY 20 JUNE 1987

I write on Herbie's birthday card, 'To the best brother in the world.' I give it to him with a big hug and bite back my emotion. I wonder for the umpteenth time when this sense of loss will subside and how Ron is feeling.

I stand awkwardly in the hall and say goodbye to them all.

Mum steps forward. 'Bye Ju, I hope you soon sort yourself out.'

I give her a hug then brace myself as Tom reaches up to give me a wet kiss. He giggles self-consciously. 'Look after yourself.'

A stab of yearning as I remember this is Ron's parting shot. I get back in my car and prepare myself for what's in store for me in the next few days.

The sunny two-hour drive begins to lighten my mood and I can't help wondering what it's like in Petersfield today. Unlike on the last journey, though, I have no more answers as to what I'm doing with my life.

As soon as I reach Beechwood Avenue, Mal drives up. I immediately want to turn round and drive away. Hot anger floods my body.

Christ! What is he doing here? Didn't he say I could have the place to myself?

He smiles shyly as he steps inside and goes to put the kettle on.

'I went to fill up with petrol,' he explains as he fills the tea pot. 'I took Grace down Mum's last night, so she's happy.'

I can't help thinking this is just a temporary balm for the weeping sore of unhappiness I have caused Grace. But I'm grateful I don't have to see the hurt and accusation in her eyes.

Mal and I chat over a cup of tea before he leaves for work and I try to put my feelings to one side. I sense he wants to try and get things cleared up but I feel very edgy after all that's happened.

I'm back in the same house of correction as before I went to Petersfield. It's all wrong.

'Do you think there's any chance of us getting back together?' his pleading expression sends my conscience into a fresh panic.

I knew this was coming.

I shake my head. 'No, not at the moment,' I sound very callous but the hurt I feel is too new and too raw.

'Do you still feel you want to go back to Petersfield?'

'No,' I lie, 'I'd rather his friendship than nothing at all.'

Mal nods. 'OK. I'll leave you to it. The gin and tonic's on the table.' Again that half smile as he picks up his car keys. He drives off and I feel nothing but tremendous relief.

At two o'clock my wheels crunch on the gravel outside Windy Ridge Kennels. A cacophony of barking – all the dogs are hoping I'm their owner come to collect them. Marjorie comes to the door, bursting with energy, in her dirty faded track suit with dogs hairs all over it. She's so jolly it's impossible to be miserable in her company. She makes me a cup of coffee and we sit in her shabby lounge. Her bloodhound lumbers in dribbling goo all over the place and I shy away from him.

Marjorie giggles, 'Not used to dogs, Julie?'

I shake my head.

'He doesn't mean any harm. It's what bloodhounds do, I'm afraid!' She listens patiently to my story; it helps me put things in perspective. I play her Ron's reassuring tape message that he gave me when I picked him up from Heathrow. I listen to his familiar voice with longing – how did we ever decide to part?

'Hi Julie, it's me, Ron. Nice to get the opportunity to talk to you again and not have to worry about who's listening in.... Oh, God, when you broke the news to me about Mal finding out about us, when he went off his brain, you wouldn't believe how I was feeling? I was so scared for you. In fact, I broke down in front of Claudette, so now she's upset and we've all gone through the same bloody... fight. But the thing with Claudette and I is that things have been getting bad for some time and it's just gotta come to an end. Mal and Grace've got the rest of their lives to live, so has she, so have us.

'Geez I'm looking forward to getting back and seeing you again. It's nice talking to you on the phone but unfortunately, phones are very limited, just a cold piece of plastic. It's not... not the same as being there with you, hugging you.'

No. Oh, I wish.

I glance at Marjorie. She smiles but she's completely engrossed in Ron's words, as am I. Even her bloodhound has sat down and appears to be listening.

'Andrew's been talking today of his plans for expanding the business, blah, blah. But er...I'm not sure when to tell him about my plans to leave Australia I might...I don't know...there's still money coming in, I've got a large estate car I'm driving around in so I might delay telling him. I've got a lot of things to sell – got records to sell, got the boat, a dinghy, an outboard motor...but you know all of this. Got a lot of stuff in the garage to sort out, so the estate car will come in very handy.... Fourteen years of hoarding!... See what you're doing to me?... You can straighten me out that way!'

'Oh, our future, mate! Doesn't it look bright, and beautiful?'

If only..

'Hello, I'm getting dried up for things to say!'

Marjorie and I exchange smiles. I can tell she's warmed to his character.

'Oh, I wish you were here,'

Yes, I do. With all my heart.

'It's just coming up to six thirty on the Friday night. And I've been humping, large heavy boxes on my own all day. I don't think my muscles have been put through so much strain in their life. I ache. Still, keeps me fit. Maybe even tone up my body a bit! You don't wanna see some fat, flabby thing....not used to fat flabby things! (a chuckle) I won't say any more about that!'

Marjorie shrieks with laughter and shakes her head. 'Oh, Julie!'

We carry on listening. Until...

'I've set my plans, I've made my decision, my future's ahead of me and you're part of it.'

(pause)

'CORRECTION! You're not A part of it, you are THE part of it, the major part.'

I stop the tape; I can't listen any more.

How could he have been that positive? The overriding issue for him now is being able to find work. He must feel worthless. He's never had this before. He was riding high in Australia.

What have I done to him? Is this all my fault?

I'm still talking about Ron while I blow-dry Marjorie's hair. She shakes her head. 'Oh, Julie. Why did you leave?'

Her sympathy tugs at my heartstrings. I can't answer her.

I follow Marjorie outside to find her old caravan covered in green algae. When she opens the door, it smells damp and musty. There are a lot of dusty old curtains and bedding rolled up in a heap, and I recoil from the thought of trying to make my home in there. I use her bathroom before I leave – the shower curtain is black with mildew, the shower head is hanging off, and there are dead leaves and mud on the bath mat. The basin is in need of a good clean and the thought of having to use this on a daily basis and sleep in the caravan is more than I can endure. But Marjorie has been kind enough to think of me. I thank her and say I'll let her know.

I will just have to make do with sleeping in my red and white cell until I find a flat to rent. I'm really looking forward to that – at least living on my own I will know where my destiny lies.

Indoors, standing on the dining table, is the G and T. It's reaching out to me, like the DRINK ME bottle in *Alice in Wonderland*. I put it away in the cupboard. I don't want anything of Mal's.

I drive to Royston for chicken and chips, come home and eat it ravenously straight out of the paper.

For a little woman, you're good on the fang.

I listen to the soundtrack of *The Trap*, with a glass of wine. The beautiful music fills me up and bathes my soul.

Every time you play this, you'll think of me.

SUNDAY 21 JUNE 1987

My mind runs straight back to Ron when I wake up. I stay around the house all day feeling desperate. I can't see any way out of this mess. Coming back was a retrograde step. I mentally shake myself.

This isn't how Ron would want me to be. I will have to be more positive in future and get on with my life.

I start making plans for the week ahead and write a to-do list.

But all too soon my freedom comes to an end when I hear the car drive up. Mal and Grace come in. I look at the clock. Midnight. Where did the time go? Grace pokes her head round the door and says a brief 'hello' then runs upstairs to bed. She doesn't look very happy to see me and I wonder how we will ever be able to heal this rift.

MONDAY 22 JUNE 1987

Mal doesn't have the day off as promised, so I escape to Royston and trawl the estate agents for properties to rent. There are very few and they're all too expensive but I feel better for trying.

I come back and ring Ron, hoping for a little praise and sympathy. But it's not forthcoming. I ask if he got the job he went for.

'Nah. They said I was over-qualified this time.'

'But that's ridiculous!'

'Yeah. I'm going back to Australia at the earliest opportunity,' he shouts.

No! Don't go, not yet.

I close my eyes and almost whisper. 'When do you think that'll be?'

I hear him sigh and chew his lip. 'I d'know yet. A mate of mine might have some removal work for me. I'll let you know. Keep in touch and I'll keep in touch. I'll send your camera back either today or tomorrow.'

Mal and I go for a walk in the evening. We talk about going out more together to see if this puts us back on the right track. Also, he's going to the Isle of Wight on Thursday and says he'll drop me off in Petersfield to collect my camera. This sounds brave of him under the circumstances, but I can't go back, not yet. I don't want to send out the wrong signals. And what sort of reception would I get? I'm on my guard now. It's best left as it is.

WEDNESDAY 24 JUNE 1987

I ring Ron but he's so distant I may as well be talking to the man in the moon. He says he's got a removal job on Friday; getting cash in hand jobs because he doesn't want to have to pay tax and national insurance. As far as the DHSS are concerned, they don't know he's here, so he can't get any benefits.

'Can't you try?'

'Nah. There would be too many questions asked.'

I have never gone into these details with him. I never realised he would be in this difficulty and feel powerless to suggest what to do.

'I'm feeling quite depressed, not my usual up-beat self.'

'I know what you mean, I'm the same. I've got a lawn looking at me – needs cutting.'

'Well, don't talk about it, do it. You'll feel better if you do something.'

I'm dismissed. I put the phone down and get out the lawn mower. Ron's right; it does help. I come in and compile another letter to my customers, feeling quite confident that most will come back to me. I knock on Susan's door and ask her to type them up for me. She's pleased to see me and sympathizes with me over a cup of tea.

'Oh, Julie, how awful for you. Do you think it'll be better when you find a flat?'

I nod. 'It can't be any worse. I keep looking but there's not much about.'

'Don't worry. Something will turn up.'

I immediately take the letter to Royston to have it photocopied, buy thirty-seven stamps and post them. The sun is shining and I'm beginning to feel more positive as if the whole episode with Ron never happened.

Mal is working away in the evening. I grab the opportunity to do some bonding with Grace and take a leaf out of Ron's book – I take her to the Beefeater, at Trumpington. I look around at the standard decor and remember Ron sitting opposite me in the Beefeater in Petersfield – it seems so long ago. I sit opposite Grace but she still finds it difficult open up to me. She's on the point of tears when I ask about her dad and how the two of them have been coping.

'You know what he's like.'

Of course I do but I'm not in a position to take her side.

What a God-awful mess.

When I look up she's picking at her food, as if every mouthful's is a struggle.

It's too public in here; I should've cooked a meal at home.

I try to put her at ease and ask her about Claire and what they've been doing but she's reluctant to talk. She pushes her half-finished meal aside and we leave.

Back at Melbourn, I pour myself a glass of Rosemount Chardonnay and try to relax. Grace, still unwilling to talk, escapes to her bedroom. I switch on the TV but it washes over me.

THURSDAY 25 JUNE 1987

My camera comes back along with some forwarded post. But no letter. Disappointment weighs me down.

I try to have another positive day and change my address back to Melbourn at the bank, the accountant, and the AA. I go round to do Jean's hair. She shows me into her pastel pink and green lounge with antique furniture and tasteful paintings. She makes a pot of Earl Grey and my thoughts immediately fly to Ron.

'No one comes right across the world for you if there's nothing there to start with, Julie.' She says in her old-mother-hen tone. 'Don't forget him.'

I'll NEVER forget him!

'Once you're on your own things will sort themselves out. Write to him, tell him how you feel.'

'Do you think I should?'

'Yes, I do. The poor man doesn't know where he is with you.'

I begin to form the words in my head then my thoughts turn to Mal. I don't know how much to tell Jean – it might get back to him through Jim. Luckily, she senses this.

'Mal's a good man, Julie,' she says in her sympathetic tone. 'He wouldn't kick a dead dog in the road, but you mustn't let that cloud everything. He'll make his own life when all this has died down. You need to let Ron know how you feel. Write and tell him. He's frightened, Julie. He offered you the moon but can't give you a starlet.'

'What if I'd stayed and started my own business, do you think it would've have helped?'

She looks me straight in the eye. 'No,' she says vehemently, 'it would have been a blow to his pride if you had to keep him.'

I wash and blow-dry Jean's hair while she tells me her daughter Mandy and her husband have come back from Ireland – he has been offered a good job here in England and they're trying to find somewhere to live. In the meantime, they're living with Jean and Jim.

'I expect they're finding it difficult, settling back here?' I ask.

She gives me a sideways look in the mirror. 'Yes, it's not easy. We all have our preferences, Julie. Different characters... but I expect something will turn up. Anyway, you don't want to hear about someone else's problems – you've got enough of your own!'

This makes me smile. I put the finishing touches to her short blonde hair and spray it.

'That's lovely, Julie. Do you think it could do with a cut next time?'

'Yes, I'll make a note.'

'Think about what I've said. Let me know when you hear from Ron.'

I walk home analysing Jean's advice on the way. Perhaps she's right about Ron. Half of me wants to believe we can get back together in the future but the other half is telling me it's finished. I don't know which half to listen to.

I come in and phone about a rented flat in Cambridge. But it's £173 a month. This seems a lot but I desperately need to get out. I tell the man I'll ring back when I can make arrangements to view.

In the evening, I ring Shirley and we go to The Plough at Shepreth for a drink. She can't believe what's happened and can't find a reason why, except Ron was worried about not finding a job. I tell Shirley about sex being very half-hearted too. Like me, she can't understand it. At least I have some very good friends who are all routing for me.

Remember. Friendship means everything.

FRIDAY 26 JUNE 1987

Jean phones in the morning. 'You're both suffering from guilty consciences, Julie – Ron with Claudette, you with Mal. You *must* write to him. Do it now!'

There's something in what she said. I don't quite know what I'm going to write, but write I will.

I go out to do a perm at ten o'clock, come back for a bite to eat and write my letter to Ron in the afternoon – nothing sloppy, just that I'm thinking of him and I'm looking for a flat to rent. And maybe we can get together in the future. I go and post it.

Mal comes home in the evening. Grace is babysitting for Mal's mate in the next road whose wife disappeared and left him holding the baby, literally.

I'm not the only one with problems.

Mal takes me out for a meal at The John Barleycorn at Duxford. I sit opposite him but it feels so wrong. It'll never work. We come back and play some jazz records, but I keep comparing him with Ron and the last great night we spent together. I just hope a flat comes up soon.

SUNDAY 28 JUNE 1987

Shirley's daughter, Becky, is performing in the majorettes at a village fête at Cottered today. Shirley has asked if Grace and I would like to go.

It's a very strange day; it's very hard not to think about Harting Fair with Ron. I look across at Grace – her expression reflects how I feel. But I try to enjoy the parade and take some photos of the Morris dancers. Poor Grace looks as if she wants to run away.

We come home and I cook dinner for us both. We sit in silence, the only sound coming from the cutlery on our plates. Mal comes in soon after and I wish he hadn't – I wanted to try and talk Grace round, break down her barriers, but she's flown up to her bedroom again.

Mal looks accusingly at me as if I should try harder with Grace. I'm so tired of trying and not getting anywhere, not being appreciated for my efforts.

Mal goes down the pub in the evening. When he comes back I'm upstairs writing my diary. He opens my sanctuary door, 'You're not talking much. For two people trying to get to know each other again, you don't have a lot to say.'

'There's nothing *to* say.'

He goes back downstairs and clatters about in the kitchen feeding Soot. I have forgotten all about the poor cat. I hear Mal throw the spoon in the sink and go to bed.

MONDAY 29 JUNE 1987

I'm busy most of the day. Fortunately, most of my customers have come back to me. The more I work, the better I feel. It's therapy.

I ring some more agencies about flats but they're either too expensive or too far away. I pray something comes up soon; I'm getting desperate.

There's a phone call from one of Mal's relatives in the afternoon telling me his Uncle Mac in Scotland has died. I tell him when he comes in. Jean's dead dog comment comes back to me. Poor man, I feel sorry for him but am powerless to console him.

I go to view a flat in Trumpington in the evening but it's very expensive and would mean sharing with a man and I'm not into that. It's also too far away. I need to be near Grace if I'm to rescue what's left of our mother/daughter relationship.

TUESDAY 30 JUNE 1987

Mal left for Scotland this morning and picked his father up on the way. The funeral is tomorrow.

The house to myself, yes!

It's a warm sunny day. I stretch out on the sun-lounger in the afternoon and watch the cotton wool clouds float by. I picture the same clouds in Petersfield.

Grace is babysitting in the next road this evening so I take the opportunity to phone Ron. I have to know if he received my letter and hope he doesn't think it sounded pathetic.

'No, of course not. You've got a good head on your shoulders. How *is* my little Vegemite?'

'Oh, all right. Some days better than others. I'd be far happier if I could find a flat.'

'Yeah, you're going through the same as what I'm going through, looking for work. How's Mal?'

'He's OK but his Uncle Mac died so he's gone to Scotland for the funeral.'

'Oh, poor bugger.'

Still that empathy; it's as if he's accusing me of being callous.

'Got a lot of removals to do at the moment, keeping me fit! You never know, I might lose a bit of weight!'

We chuckle.

How I miss you.

'Oh, guess what? I've got a tax cheque coming from Australia so I've got my plane ticket sorted out!'

Oh God, no. Not yet.

I try to sound happy for him but I can't bring myself to ask when he's going. I'm on the point of asking him how he feels about me now, but one of his mates comes round for him.

'Listen, I've gotta go. I'll phone you tomorrow at nine.'

Where do all these 'mates' come from? I've never seen any of them.

WEDNESDAY 1 JULY 1987

Ron keeps his word and rings dead on nine. I take a deep breath and ask him how he feels about me now. I've been fretting about this all night.

'Well, I still like you a heck-of-a-lot, but if you're asking me where my heart lies, it's in Australia. My mind keeps wandering back to Canberra and Sydney.'

A 'heck-of-a- lot'? He used these same words in 1967. A heavy sigh escapes me. I swallow hard. 'You won't go back to Australia without seeing me, will you?'

'No, of course not! I couldn't do that. Anyhow, I'm not going till October when I've got the money together.'

In the hall mirror, I watch my shoulders relax. Ironically, this same mirror showed me how happy I was to get that first phone call way back in January.

'I'll write to you answering your letter. In the meantime, it's Dad's birthday on Saturday so we're giving him a surprise party! Can't wait to see his face!'

'How lovely, I wish I could be there.'

He doesn't offer any sympathy or ask me to go. It seems life in Petersfield is still going on without me.

'Anyhow, gotta go. Catch you later.'

In the evening, Grace is at the visiting fun-fair in the village and Mal's still in Scotland – he rang earlier to say he was having such a good time, he might stay for another two weeks!

Hurrah!

But that would be too good to be true. I walk round to see Rowena, another customer in Water Lane, and take her hairspray she ordered. She asks me in for a cup of tea, wants to hear my news. She's also good to talk to and as usual, I can't stop talking about Ron. I'm lucky I have such patient and understanding friends.

I come back home at nine and I watch an Australian film called *The Far Country*. It fascinates me. In fact, I have a morbid fascination for anything Australian and want to find out all I can about the country. Maybe someday I'll be lucky enough to go.

Grace comes in and runs up to her room. I pour myself a glass of wine and watch twenty five years of *Island Records*. I sit listening to all the old greats – Steve Winwood, Bob Marley, Traffic, Marianne Faithful – and wonder if Ron is watching it.

I hear the front door open behind me. It's Mal. My resentment rises; I thought he was staying in Scotland a bit longer. He takes one look at me and his face drops. He pours himself a whisky and slumps in the armchair. I go up to bed to escape his self pity. I'm done with all that.

FRIDAY 3 JULY 1987

Our big black cat Soot looks a sorry sight this morning. He hasn't been eating for the last few days and his belly is bloated. It doesn't bode well. Mal takes him to the vet's and when he comes back he gives me the terrible news – Soot has cancer of the liver. Mal looks at me as if it's my fault.

'The vet was going to put him down there and then but I couldn't face it, especially as Grace hasn't had a chance to say goodbye to him. I told the vet I'll take him back on Monday.'

'But he's suffering!'

'Huh, yeah.'

The unspoken words 'like me' hang in the air.

Grace is heartbroken when she comes in from school. She's grown up with Soot. I remember when we got him.

We had a mouse problem in the three-room flat we rented in Nunhead when Grace was a baby. The traps couldn't keep up with the demand – we used to lie in bed and listen to them going off. Mal would get up and reset them and this would go on all night. Mal was more of a dog person, so I jumped at the chance when he told me to get a cat. I went out in my lunch-hour the next day and spotted a little ball of black fluff for £2.50 in the covered market in Rye Lane. The kitten was all on his own, the stallholder insisting the others had all been sold. Whether or not this was a marketing ploy, I didn't care. I took the six-week old kitten back to work in a cardboard box with instructions on how to look after him. He was a great distraction – all the girls in the salon made a big fuss of him, preferring to play with the kitten instead of working. When I took him home, Mal took one look at him and said, 'How's a thing that small gonna catch mice?'

But I smiled to myself when, late in the evening, Mal put a pair of fur mittens next to him to imitate his mother, and left the kitchen light on for him all night. We called him Sooty because he was as black as coal but his name very soon got shortened to Soot.

222

He grew up to be a fighter even though we had him neutered. He was fiercely territorial and if any other cat dared to enter our garden he would fly at it, both of them locked in mortal combat, until the other cat limped away licking its wounds. On one occasion, I tried to part them but Soot went for me! These fights resulted in frequent trips to the vet to lance his abscesses. We had a job to keep up with the bills so I watched the vet and learned how to bathe Soot's wounds. Soot strangely enough, did not protest.

When we moved to Melbourn, Jean came round one day and saw Soot enjoying the sunny garden. She remarked that he thought it was a lovely place to retire to! He mellowed into a big cat with a great character. If Grace was doing her homework on the floor, he'd go and sit on her papers in front of her, making her take notice of him. He was always with Grace. She will miss him dreadfully.

SATURDAY 4 JULY 1987

Grace is in Cambridge with friends and Mal's cleaning cars. Poor Soot is looking very sorry for himself but there's nothing I can do for him. I pack a bag and drive to Mum's for the weekend to leave the house of misery behind me.

I sun-bathe in Mum's little garden and watch Herbie and Bridget relaxing on a rug on the grass. Both in their twenties, I'm envious of their youth and their new-found love and in my mind I liken them to a pair of fawns frolicking in a wood.

I ring Jack in Petersfield to wish him happy birthday. 'Are you doing anything for it?' I know, of course, that a special birthday surprise has been planned.

'Probably be watching telly! Want to speak to Mum?'

I tell Lottie about Soot. 'Oh, dear, I'm sorry to hear that. I love my cat. I don't know what I'd do if anything happened to him. Ron's gone to a fête for something to do. I think he's at a bit of a loose end. How are you, love?'

'I'm OK. At Mum's for the weekend. The weather's lovely here. I expect we'll go out later.'

'That's good, love. Well, thanks for phoning. I'll tell Ron you rang.'

In the evening, I go with Mum and Tom, Herbie and Bridget, to Grove Ferry, a pretty pub on a river. Coloured lights shining on the water. Boats everywhere, river trips. It's inevitable that I think of Ron. Boats always remind me of him – I know it will always be the same. I try to imagine the scene in Petersfield and Jack's face when they surprise him with the birthday get-together. I shiver, pull my jacket tighter and wrap my arms around my body.

SUNDAY 5 JULY 1987

Tom's at work at the children's home so I spend the day with Mum, just the two of us. It's been a long time since we've done that. Not that I was ever a mummy's girl, far from it. Dad was my shining light as far back as I can remember. I spent weekends with him in the garden during the long hot summers, watching him lovingly tend his plants and manicure the lawns. On wet days I would watch him draw and paint and ask him to draw me something to colour in. I remember him painting my portrait while I sat in the hot conservatory trying not to fidget. All these images locked securely away in my scrapbook of memories. But Mum was always there in the background ready to administer medicine and plasters and all things maternal. I'm thankful her health seems stable now; one less worry. She never makes any fuss, takes it all in her stride, and I marvel at her bravery.

In the morning we go to a boot fair. The sun is beating down on my arms and I've forgotten the sun cream. We don't buy anything but enjoy pawing over the second-hand items, having our memories jogged with things we once owned. We go for a drink at *The Nineteenth Hole* at lunchtime. Mum listens to me talk about Ron again. I get the feeling she has very little grasp of the situation, but it's comforting when she nods in all the right places.

We go to Broadstairs in the afternoon and I get sunburnt walking along the prom. We buy ice creams in the 1950s ice cream parlour. I bask in the cosy memories of family holidays long past.

I leave it till nine-thirty to drive home, hoping to avoid the traffic, but the cars are nose to tail on the M2. I sit listening to *Phantom.* After an hour I realise I've only achieved thirty miles. Then, a break in the traffic and I decide to turn off the motorway towards Faversham and take the old A2 through the Medway towns. I instantly remember my way from years ago when Rose and Steve lived at Chatham. Ron's spirit is at my shoulder spurring me on as I keep imagining what he would do in this situation. Turn it into an experience, of course. I even fantasize about staying at a country house for the night, but decide against it.

The journey that usually takes two hours has taken me four. I arrive home to a dark and silent house and give myself a mental pat on the back. But in a bizarre way, I've enjoyed the experience and feel exhilarated as I creep up the stairs.

MONDAY 6 JULY 1987

At nine o'clock in the morning Mal takes Soot to the vet's to have him put down. Grace said her goodbye before she went to school, while I stayed out of the way. I couldn't bring myself to witness such sadness. Soot looks a very sorry sight as Mal places him carefully in the cat basket, his belly swollen to twice its normal size and his tongue poking out. But we all know it's the only way. Nothing can be done for him now.

I go about my work with a dark cloud hanging over me. I loved Soot, and this is another terrible blow for me. I come back at lunchtime to find Mal has buried him on the rockery, without me. I stand on my own, looking at the little mound of fresh earth and wait for the tears to come. I can't define how I feel. Guilty, I suppose, as though Soot's death is partly my fault but logically, I know I could not have caused his cancer.

When I turn round Mal is there. 'He looked so peaceful when I brought him back. At least *he's* been put out of his misery.'

I find this pathetic remark over the top and walk back indoors.

Grace goes to the school disco in the evening. She seems to have come to terms with Soot's death and is even talking about getting another kitten. But there will never be another Soot.

Mal fires up the barbecue. I open a chilled bottle of Rosemount Chardonnay and the memory of the wine bar in Petersfield opens up before me. I eat my food on automatic pilot. The Australian wine goes down a treat and we walk down to the off-licence and buy another bottle. I'm amazed that Mal doesn't openly make the connection with Ron and the wine, but maybe he ignores it for my sake. I'm in a drunken stupor when Mal goes to collect Grace. It's my way of escaping.

WEDNESDAY 8 JULY 1987

The situation at home is getting worse and Marjorie's caravan is looking more and more inviting. Grace has left my hot brush outside her bedroom door this morning. I have been using it in her bedroom as the electric point is near the mirror. She only speaks to me if she has to.

A letter from Ron drops on the mat. I can't believe the content – it's so blunt.

G'day mate,

Hope you are sorting yourself out OK.

I did 17 hrs straight yesterday, shifting furniture and got home at 1am. I am writing this just before leaving for the I.O.W. which will probably be another14 hr day. Please find enclosed your mail.

I've decided that October is when I fly back to Australia, so all I am going to do is casual work through the summer, I am forgetting about management jobs here.

I hope things will work out for you and Mal. I'm sure it will. Only time will tell.

I really can't put a finger on why it didn't work out between us. When it boils down to it, it seems that we were both going through the same domestic situation and we both utilised our meeting after 20 yrs as a way out.

We both succeeded in hurting people like Mal, Grace and Claudette, but if Mal is understanding which I'm sure he will be, you could both sort your futures out.

I've got my sorting out with Claudette to try in October but things will have to work in a different way than the old situation.

Got to fly,

Look after yourself. Thinking of you.
Ron.

I put the letter back in the envelope and wonder momentarily if I should take Ron's advice. But I can't face it. This is one suggestion of Ron's I am not going to act on.

In the evening, Mal's working away and Grace is babysitting, so I take the opportunity to ring Ron and thank him for his letter.

'I've been in touch with Claudette and it looks like I'll be in the same situation as you when I get back. If it doesn't work out with her, she'll be expecting me to move out.'

I'm struck dumb.

If it doesn't work out with her?

'Yeah, I don't know. You should ask Mal what he wants you to do. Don't try to make things happen – it will sort itself out.'

'I hope you're right.' There's a pause and I know he's trying to think what else to say. 'I've been thinking about what went wrong with us,' he says. 'I think things would have been different if we'd had a courting period.'

'I think so, too. It didn't have time to develop; we needed more time, something we didn't have.'

No. Never enough time.

He sighs and takes another deep breath; sounds like he's taking mouthfuls of beer in between. 'I've been shifting a lot of furniture, getting fit. Down to fourteen stone now, and getting brown.'

'Ha, browned off!'

'Huh, yeah.'

I try to imagine what he looks like now and wonder if he thinks I found his weight repulsive.

There's another pause, then, 'Sometimes I think I'll stay and other times I want to go back. Anyhow, I'll keep in touch.'

FRIDAY 10 JULY 1987

I feel very negative. I wish I knew what I was doing with my life. I keep thinking about Ron. He's with me in everything I do as if we're joined by an invisible thread. Maybe he's right and I should try harder with Mal, but the prospect frightens me. I can't commit to Mal and close the door on maybe another chance of a future with Ron.

I see Mal's heavy bulk bent over the newspaper on the table. A cup of tea by his side. For a moment I'm reminded of Ron doing the same. I open my mouth but no words come out. He looks round at me. A half smile. He's not sure how to treat me, what to say.

'All right?' he manages.

I nod and brace myself. 'I need to talk to you. Don't look so worried, it's nothing nasty.'

I sit at the other end of the table to create space between us. 'I've been thinking. We need to try and do something positive. That way...'

His smile broadens. 'Yeah, why not? If we go out more and do things together...?'

I nod, but while he is visibly uplifted by this, the prospect weighs heavily on me.

He takes me to the golf range at Whaddon. I don't know why he thinks I'll be interested in whacking a load of golf balls into a net, but he pays for a bucket of balls and proceeds to show me what to do. I find it easy, maybe it's beginners luck but with each ball I relieve my tension, despair and anger. Apart from that, I find it a pointless exercise. We come to the end of the bucket and he puts it away. All is conducted in silence until he suggests we have a drink at The Plough at Shepreth. New people have taken it over and there are tubs of flowers in the newly-paved garden with a barbecue that takes pride of place. We sit outside awkward with each other, like two people on a first date. We skirt round the subject of getting back together. Neither of us is able to take that leap it seems.

It's still warm when we come back and we sit on the patio with another drink; a whiskey for him and a gin and tonic for me. Next door, Susan and Colin are getting ready for bed. Noises of water running coming from their bathroom and lights being switched on in the bedroom.

Mal looks up at their bedroom window. 'Everyone expects different things from a relationship – take them next door. They seem quite simple and uncomplicated; they've probably had sex a few times and got two kids out of it, and are quite happy with that.'

Does he really believe that? Am I expecting too much? Is that the trouble with Ron and me? Did we expect too much?

When I look at Mal my heart sinks. This is never going to work. After half an hour of silence we say goodnight without any physical contact and go our separate ways.

SATURDAY 11 JULY 1987

I take Grace to Cambridge for the day; she still needs shoes. We are more successful this time – we buy the school shoes then find ourselves in Andy's Records. Grace goes to the record section while I'm drawn to the shelf of tapes and find The Moody Blues albums. *The Other Side of Life* leaps out at me, begging me to buy it. I read the play list. *Your Wildest Dreams* is the first track! As I clutch the tape to me, my skin prickles with excitement and I my throat constricts. It even has the lyrics printed on the inside cover. Grace buys a Duran Duran album and we come home.

Mal is indoors. I'm itching to play my tape so I take it into the car, hoping he doesn't ask any questions. I turn it on and play it softly in case, in some peculiar way, he knows what it means to me. My eyes are moist; my heart is so full of love for Ron I could burst.

In the evening, still looking for things to do together, Mal and I go to a jazz concert at the Meridian School in Royston. It turns out to be modern jazz. Mal is disapproving but I can appreciate their skill. I keep glancing at him, testing myself, and realize I have no feelings for him whatsoever. We leave halfway through the performance and go straight home. There's no goodnight kiss; he doesn't ask and I'm relieved.

SUNDAY 12 JULY 1987

Mal's at work in the morning and Grace is upstairs listening to Madonna with her bedroom door closed. I listen to the Moody Blues tape. I plug my headphones into the sound system, the music fills my head and am instantly transported back to that first day with Ron, watching that wonderful video. Icy goose bumps run over my body. It's like a drug, I can't get enough. I will never forget Ron; he is too much part of me now.

I go out to fill up with petrol and play the tape again. I'm riding on a high. I wonder if Ron's heard the album; I must ask him. I would like to know if he thinks the lyrics to the rest of the album portray our story.

I come home and cut the lawn and cook lunch. Mal comes in and I can't look at him. After our meal he suggests we go and buy some plants for the garden. I half-heartedly agree. I wander around the garden centre thinking only of Ron and nodding to anything Mal suggests.

We come back and I immediately run up to my sanctuary.

Mal bursts in and shouts, 'You don't have to make it so blatantly obvious you're in a mood. I just thought it would be something to do. What's the use? You're kidding yourself when you say you wanna make a new start, you knew last night. You should've stayed in Petersfield. You're on the move again, aren't you?'

I turn my wet eyes to him. He turns away and storms downstairs. I close the door behind him, write my diary and fall asleep.

In the evening Mal asks me to go to the Cambridge Motel with him where we can sit outside and talk. Over a couple of glasses of wine we agree that the best thing for me to do is to find a flat so I can live on my own. I'm so relieved I could kiss him but that would only complicate matters again.

MONDAY 13 JULY 1987

I wake up and pray to God I find a flat soon. Two things could come out of this – I would have my freedom and I could get back with Ron on a more even keel and do things properly this time. It all happened far too quickly; we didn't give ourselves a chance. I want to write to Ron and tell him but I'm frightened of his reaction. I know he's hell bent on going back to Australia and only hope he'll let me know when. The thought of him slipping away without my seeing him again is destroying me.

I walk into the village at lunchtime and buy the *Royston Crow*. I sit on a bench at the side of the road, in the sun, and turn to the accommodation page. One boxed advert leaps out at me – 'Lady wanted to share house in Royston. £30 a week.' I run home and ring the number. A woman called Carol answers. She sounds very pleasant and asks me round to view it tonight.

Yes! At last I'm getting somewhere.

At 5:30 I drive into Minster Road with trepidation. What I'm doing is totally alien to me but here goes. I park the Nova and look around; it's a cul-de-sac with a few semi-detached houses. The last one in the row looks the best-kept with hanging baskets of mixed petunias and a tub of red geraniums at the door. I walk into the little front garden and knock. I'm met with a sparkly smile. Carol's a petite natural blonde and although she's wearing jeans, she has a well-turned-out appearance. Her border collie looks at me with soulful eyes. Carol tells the dog to go and lie down. She cowers, nose to floor and slumps in her bed under the stairs.

'Come in,' says Carol, standing to one side. 'Julie, is it?'

'That's right.'

She ushers me into her spotless front room. She motions to a large beige armchair. I sit down, not knowing where to start.

Carol realises my discomfort. 'Cup of tea?'

'That would be nice. Thanks.'

She quickly goes through the beaded curtain to the kitchen. I hear her fill the kettle and switch it on. She comes back with the black and white dog in tow. 'Come in, Tess.' She sits down and pats the dog. 'Do you like dogs, Julie?'

I nod but I sense Tess is aware I'm not a dog person. She licks Carol's hand whilst looking up at me with big brown eyes.

'So,' says Carol, 'How long will you be needing the room?'

'Indefinitely' comes to mind but I decide against it. 'I'm not sure at the moment.'

'That's fine.'

She excuses herself and goes to make the tea. Tess follows nervously. I take another look around and decide the décor is more suited to an older person; everything is brown and beige. There are old-fashioned pictures on the walls and pot plants on various stands. In the other half of the room there's a glass-topped dining table with tubular steel chairs. In one corner, a music centre stands on a chest of drawers. I assume the net-curtained window looks out onto the back garden.

Carol comes back with two mugs of tea on a tray with sugar and milk. 'How do you take it?'

'Just milk, thanks.'

She hands me the red and white mug and places a coaster on the coffee table next to me.

'Thanks.'

I'm being over polite.

Carol proceeds to tell me the rent is £30 a week and she prefers me to pay in cash, if that's OK? I have no problem with that; it will hardly make a dent in my weekly takings.

'Would you like to see the room?'

I follow her up the beige-carpeted stairs and she shows me the double bedroom at the back of the house. It's decorated mainly in blue and white and looks very clean. The pink bathroom is next door.

I notice the blanket box under the window which would be perfect for all my hairdressing equipment. 'I'm happy to pay the phone bill, too, as I'll need it for my business.'

'Oh? What business is that?'

'I'm a mobile hairdresser.'

I can see she's thinking a resident hairdresser would be an advantage.

'Well, you don't have to pay the bill. I'm sure we can come to some arrangement?'

But I'm adamant; it means I can use the phone whenever I want without feeling guilty. 'No. I would rather pay it. I'd feel much happier that way.'

'OK, if you're sure?'

I nod and follow her back downstairs to the living room. Take a sip of my cooled tea.

'When do you want to move in?'

'As soon as possible,' I want to say but don't want to sound too eager. 'Would next Sunday be all right?'

She nods and chucks Tess under the chin. 'I'd like a week's rent in advance. Let me know what time you want to come. Sunday's a good day for me. I'm at my mum's for dinner but apart from that I'm usually here.'

With the formalities out of the way we both begin to relax.

I decide to let her know my position. 'I'm separated from my husband, and I've got a daughter, Grace. She's fifteen. She'll be living with her dad.' It's as though someone else has spoken for me.

Carol nods again. 'I'm divorced, so we've got something in common.' She smiles widely showing a perfect set of white teeth. She pats Tess as a kind of security blanket and I get the impression she's uncomfortable with her situation. 'I'm in the ambulance service so I work different shifts. I'm hoping to get my ambulance driver's licence soon, then promotion,' she says, excitedly.

Couldn't be better – much needed space to myself.

'You can use the house as your own. I don't mind as long as you keep it clean and tidy.'

'Of course.'

I feel the interview has come to an end so I stand up. Carol also stands. 'Well, I'll see you on Sunday, Julie. You've got my number?'

I nod. 'Yeah, thanks.'

This is all very strange but I have the feeling it's going to suit me very well; it's what I've been waiting for – I can do what I want, when I want, without worrying about Grace and Mal's feelings. The house is ideal. I come away feeling I've made progress. Next Sunday can't come soon enough.

I go home and tell Mal.

'Well, if that's what you want. But it's got to be said; When, or **if** you come back, next time it's got to be as a wife, *not* a lodger.'

This goes without saying. I also know I'll never be coming back. Not to live anyway.

I write to Ron telling him I've found a place to rent, give him the address and phone number. I harbour the hope that we can start seeing see each other again when I've moved.

TUESDAY 14 JULY 1987

I've got my photos back from *Truprint* of Ron on Butser Hill and a lovely one of the sun glinting through the trees in Buriton. I'm instantly transported back to that day. If only things had worked out but that was the other side of life, like the title of the Moody Blues album. I listen to it at every available opportunity, mostly in the car travelling between clients. I talk about Ron incessantly and they ask how I'm getting on. I thank my lucky stars I have such caring friends but none of them have ever met him. It's as if he's a figment of my imagination.

There's a letter from Ron:

Hi Jules,

Hope you are continuing to sort yourself out. I am not working at the moment, the furniture removal co. Docked 50 quid out of my wages towards the damage to their lorry. I jammed it under a bridge. The thing that really gave me the shits was they didn't tell me first so we could've worked something out. So I told them to stick the job.

I have booked my ticket for Australia on 18th August, but if my trunk arrives and I sort everything out earlier, I will definitely get an earlier flight.

Things between Claudette and me look as if it could start again. I've certainly changed my outlook on life since I've been in this country.

Now you have found a house to share you will find that things will begin to work out for you and live the life you want.

I won't forget you. And every now and again I'll read your little poem and think of you fondly and often and you will always hold a special place in my heart.

All the best for you in the future. I hope it all works out.

Ron.

I slump in the armchair as the words sink in.

He expects to get back together with Claudette. He might go back even sooner.

A chill sweeps over my body at the thought.

I ring Jean. She asks me round for lunch and I show her the letter. She stops what she's doing in the kitchen and reads it intently. We wander into her sitting room.

She looks up. 'This man is a coward, Julie. He's running away. He's not for you.'

'But he says he'll keep a special place in his heart for me.'

'Big deal! He's doing the same to you as he did to Claudette. Can't wait to get away. He's irresponsible, Julie.'

'But is he? He gave up everything to comeback to England. And me.'

Jean gives me a sideways look. 'You also gave up a lot. Don't forget that. But when you've been on your own for a few months, get your feelings sorted out, you never know. Everything could fall into place.'

WEDNESDAY 22 JULY 1987

I pick up the phone at nine. I can't leave it any longer; I've been thinking about this for hours – I have a horrible feeling Ron's going back without giving me the chance to say goodbye.

'I got your letter. Can I see you before you run back to Australia?'

He's very abrupt as if I'm an inconvenience. 'I'm going to London at the weekend to have my ticket brought forward. When I know what I'm doing, I'll ring you and arrange to meet somewhere.'

Time is running out, but I can't let emotion cloud my voice; I don't want him to know how hurt I am. 'OK. I'll wait to hear from you, then.'

I put the phone down and collapse in a heap with my head in my hands. How has the fairy tale come to this?

The phone rings again. I jump. It's Rowena. When I've booked her appointment I tell her what Ron's just said.

'Oh, dear, it must have been terrible for you. Do you think you're doing the right thing, moving out?'

'I'm sure it'll make all the difference. It's the only way for me now – I will be able to look at it in a different light if I distance myself.'

'Well, I think you're being very brave. If you need to chat, you know where I am.'

'Thanks.'

In the afternoon I have my hair highlighted at *Something Different*, the new salon in the village. Ron's with me all the time. My hair's getting longer and I hope he notices the next time I see him. I come out of the shop feeling amazing. I'll show Ron how confident I am, even though he's leaving. I must appear strong. He wouldn't want me to see me as a snivelling wreck.

THURSDAY 23 JULY 1987

I wake up with a jolt at 5am. It's no good – I'm going to have to phone and make sure I can meet him. I don't care, I *have* to see him. There are a lot of unanswered questions. I rehearse what I'm going to say in my mind to make it sound less pleading and whiney. By nine I have it all worked out and sufficient courage to pick up the phone. He sounds happy about seeing me and we arrange to meet at Trafalgar Square on Wednesday at 11am.

I go round to do Jean's hair and tell her about it.

'You'll never last out till Wednesday, Julie.'

'I know, but what can I do?'

'Phone him back and tell him. Do you want to ring from here?'

'Er....no thanks, Jean. I'll do it later.'

Jean's mantra is the same as Ron's – 'Don't talk about it, do it!' They're both Sagittarians.

I've got to do this my way. I know she's only trying to help but I want to be on my own, **if** *or* **when** *I ring him next time.*

I come in and stand by the phone, remembering how excited I was at his first phone call back in January and how terribly wrong all this is. I should be with him, we should be together living our dream. I take a deep breath and ring the number.

'Can I see you before Wednesday?'

He whistles through his teeth. 'I'm having Lofty's family over at the weekend, and if I go back it'll be the last time I see him.'

If! He said **if.**

'We should be on our own when we talk, anyway,' he says.

'Yes, I know.'

'Surely you can hang on till Wednesday?'

'I'll grin and bear it.'

He softens. 'Yeah, we've had a year of that, haven't we? What do you want to discuss?'

My stomach lurches. 'I don't want to talk about it over the phone.'

'OK. I'll see you Wednesday, then.'

'Yep, I'll be there.'

I go round to see Rowena and take the Moody Blues tape with me. We listen to it together while she makes us some lunch. She's very sympathetic and I'm grateful she has time for me in her busy family life. She carries on with the ironing while we listen to the rest of the tape.

'Do you know?' she says, 'this tape was made for you and Ron. From what you've told me, it's exactly your story.'

I have to agree — it's very poignant. We talk about the anticipated meeting over spaghetti bolognaise and I am lost in my thoughts of that day in Bungee's...

SATURDAY 25 JULY 1987

I rang Carol yesterday to confirm I would be moving in this evening instead of tomorrow. I can't wait – freedom at last, but I want to include Grace in the move. I'm hoping we can become closer and I can see her more often away from the marital home. She agrees to go with me but with little enthusiasm. I think of the day we first viewed our house – a divorced man showed us around. Now the house would have another story to tell. I had been so pleased with the house and Jean and Jim had been very helpful inviting us to dinner when we decorated the rooms prior to moving in. How quickly those four years have flown. Everything has changed and now I can't wait to move out. One thing for certain – I will never come back; not to live, anyway.

I cook dinner for the three of us which we eat in silence. I collect all my belongings together and load the car up yet again. Grace helps reluctantly in a mood that's difficult to read. She's very quiet. I make sure I have everything this time – I don't want to have to come back. Grace sits in the passenger seat while I say goodbye to Mal. He says nothing, hangs his head.

Shortly after six we arrive at Carol's. She greets us with a welcoming smile but there's no smile from Grace – she makes me feel uncomfortable without saying a word. Carol shows me up to my room – it looks very inviting – freshly cleaned and there's crisp linen on the bed and a vase of flowers on the dressing table. Already it looks like home and I'm looking forward to my first night. Grace stands awkwardly in the doorway. I quickly organise the bulk of my things, dumping the heavy bags and boxes and go downstairs. I resolve to unpack later.

Carol offers us a cup of tea but Grace shakes her head, perches on the edge of the sofa and looks down at her hands in her lap. She starts to pick her fingers. Carol tries to make conversation but the atmosphere is strained. I feel uncomfortable and sad for Grace.

'Do you want to go?' I ask her.

She nods. I take her out to the car and tell Carol I'll be back shortly.

When I open the front door, Mal's venting his anger, furiously stripping the wallpaper off the walls in the hall. Grace runs past him and upstairs. There's nothing left to say except, 'I'll phone you in a couple of weeks, or you ring me?'

'Yeah, yeah,' he moans, keeping his face to the wall.

'It's just something I've gotta do.'

He viciously scrapes at the wallpaper gouging out chunks of plaster. I feel uneasy leaving Grace.

How will they cope this time, the two of them?

I take out my key and step through Carol's front door to my new life. Tess comes to sniff at my legs. Back in the living room Carol calls her to heel. I have a good feeling about Carol.

MONDAY 27 JULY 1987

At seven I wake up to the sounds of Carol leaving for work. I briefly wonder where I am then remember the preceding day. I grab my dressing gown and go downstairs to make some breakfast in the alien red and white kitchen. Carol's divided her fridge with her food in one side and mine in the other. I acquaint myself with the cupboards and organise my space. It's very quiet, just the ticking of the heating timer in the adjacent back porch, but it's a comfortable silence. No dog. Carol's routine means that she leaves at seven every morning and takes Tess to her mum's. After work, she has dinner at her mum's, picks Tess up and comes home. This means I have the place to myself for much of the day and the run of the kitchen, which suits me down to the ground.

After breakfast I go to Cambridge to the hairdressing wholesaler's, stock up with supplies and call in to my accountant in Chesterton. On the way home I go and see how Grace is doing. Mal has punched the ranch doors off the kitchen in his temper and thrown them in a heap outside on the grass. In the space of one night the house seems hostile, broken.

Grace makes me a cup of tea. 'You don't have to see him like that. He's very upset – he cried last night.'

I don't know what to say to this. I do feel sorry for him but if he feels like this now, what would he do if, and it was a big *if*, Ron and I started seeing each other again? It's a frightening thought but I feel so empty after coming back from Petersfield. I will have to tell Ron how I feel on Wednesday. I can't let him slip through my fingers again.

TUESDAY 28 JULY 1987

I come in from work and the phone's ringing. It's Ron!

'Hi mate.'

'Hello,' I smile, 'how are you?'

'I'm afraid I can't make it tomorrow. My ticket won't be in till Friday and funds won't allow me two trips to London.'

Disappointment engulfs me, all hope of seeing him again disappearing into the distance.

'I'm using money I haven't got, now. I owe my family a lot of money. I'm going to have to pay it all back when I get to Australia. Still,' he says, cheerily, 'I've got a job to go back to already.'

My heart sinks even further. My legs go weak.

'It's so different in Australia; this country has really pissed me about. I'm looking to going back as early as next Wednesday. My mind's made up.'

NO! You can't go. Not yet.

'I'm the reason you're here,' I say in a little voice.

He corrects me. 'No, there were four reasons why I'm here and you're one of them. I'm so disillusioned with England, it's not funny.'

And what about sweet little Claudette?

He's read my mind. 'I'm not going back to Claudette, that's finished. It's my lifestyle I'm missing. I had it so good in Australia; I've *never* been out of work before.'

I've been cast aside, not for another woman but another country. How can I compete with that? 'I'll see you on Friday, then. I think I can make it.'

'OK I'll try and ring you before. I'm sorry about this but I can't afford any extra trips.'

I put the phone down and Shirley rings to cancel her appointment on Friday, and Pauline's already cancelled hers! That leaves Rowena. I ring to ask if I can change her appointment.

'Yes, of course. Oh, dear, I'm so sorry to hear that. Maybe Friday will be a better day for you?'

'Thanks. I hope so.'

I ring Jean and change her appointment.

Yes! Friday off!

It's a stroke of luck and I need plenty of that right now. I phone Ron back and arrange to meet him at Trafalgar Square at eleven o'clock. But I need a miracle to make him stay. Whatever happens, I vow to enjoy my Friday with Ron – he's taught me so much in a short time. I remember our last night together when I had been upset about the unfortunate day. He said, 'Never wish your time away. We've still got the evening to enjoy. Today might have been bad but never say, 'I can't wait for tomorrow'.'

WEDNESDAY 29 JULY 1987

I've had a good day with Grace. I took her to Cambridge this morning and cut her hair when we came back. I need to do things like this; normality is a balm for her disappointment, and mine. But of course, I have to keep this to myself. I can't tell her any of it.

I've joined a tap dancing class. I've always enjoyed dancing; it's something that relieves the tension and stops me brooding on the past. But this evening I find the Masonic hall closed. The tap class is cancelled. So I decide to cook a meal for Carol and me and splash out on a bottle of Rosemount Chardonnay. Carol's not a drinker. She politely takes a sip and says, 'Mm, that's nice,' and leaves the rest until we're eating. I tell her all about Ron and she tells me all about her divorce – her husband left her for a former girlfriend who earned the name 'Yo-Yo drawers.' I feel as if Carol is judging me in the same light as her husband. However, as the evening wears on, we begin to loosen up and make each other laugh. I'm right about Carol – we're going to get on OK. She goes up for a bath at ten and toddles off to bed while I have two more glasses of wine.

THURSDAY 30 JULY 1987

I come in from work to find Carol's left a message for me by the phone. Ron's had to cancel tomorrow – his ticket won't to be in now until Monday or Tuesday. I can't believe this – either I'm not meant to see him again, or he's not meant to go back. I ring Jean. She tells me to go to Petersfield tomorrow and see him. 'Ring him, Julie! Do it now!'

I phone Ron but he sounds angry.

'I can't wait to get on that plane!' he shouts. 'This country's really pissed me about.'

'I've got tomorrow off.'

'Well, enjoy yourself!'

'I was going to come down for the day.'

'I might have a job tomorrow, delivering carpet, which will earn me twenty-five quid. Gotta find the bloke tonight and see if it's still on. I'll phone you in the morning between nine and nine thirty, if I'm not working. If you don't hear, I've got up early and gone.'

'I've got next Wednesday off, if you're going up for your ticket that day?'

'OK I'll see you.'

I have to tell somebody. I ring Shirley.

'Oh, dear. How did he seem?'

'In his words – really pissed off! I don't know if he wants to see me or not. I just don't know what to think any more. I'm going down to my mum's a day early, sod him. If he phones, I'll tell him I'm going down there and see what reaction I get.'

'Well, I think it would be better to be with someone at the moment. Try not to think about it too much. I'm sure he won't go without you seeing him again.'

'God, I hope you're right.'

FRIDAY 31 JULY 1987

Ron didn't ring.

On the journey down to Margate I keep turning it all over in my mind. Why was this meant to happen to me? I can't believe it was all for nothing. Why did Ron bring all my feelings to the surface and yet there was no sexual desire? It's definitely a spiritual relationship but what about the physical? Would it have gone full circle if we'd had more time? I also want to know how long he's wanted to go back to Australia. I need answers on Wednesday.

SATURDAY 1 AUGUST 1987

I sit alone in Mum's little living room with a cup of coffee and read our horoscopes for the month ahead.

Aquarius: 'Around the 9th of August you will know if a relationship is meant to last. This month will make or break a partnership – view one particular involvement with more honesty and objectivity. The full moon on the 9th either means you take control of certain upsetting situations or call the whole thing a day.

Sagittarius: The last six months have been disappointing but August will make up for them. Between the 7th and 21st will stand out in your memory. Life may take some unexpected turns but they will all add up to greater happiness. Travel is particularly well starred but wherever you are you will no longer feel alone, neglected or down in the dumps. After the 23rd, your professional life is well high-lighted in a rather special way and later, success, recognition and the acceptance you crave.'

This does nothing for my optimism. It all points to Ron going back to Australia and getting on with his life.

To cheer myself up, I drive along the coast, park the car in Westgate and stroll along the sea front. The memory of happy Sundays long ago sparks a tender yearning. How simple and carefree they were! The sun is picking out the white tips of the waves and a flock of ringed plovers swoop rhythmically down and up again in front of me and land on the shiny wet sand. The air is clean and fresh after the night's ebb and flow of the tide; the day feels brand new. It's a beautiful picture and I'm reminded again how Dad loved this resort. When we lived in Bexley, we would all pile into the Anglia on a Sunday and come here for the day. But the happy memories are short-lived: this was the place where he was hoping to retire to, a dream that never became reality. A heavy feeling settles in the pit of my stomach and I bite back the tears. But then I hear Ron's voice in my ear telling me to ignore this feeling and make the most of the day.

The café is busy. I walk in and order a coffee and sit outside on one of the white plastic chairs in the sun, watching the waves. The Isle of Wight comes to mind and Ron's face is there before me. Try as I might, I am struggling to adopt his philosophy. There is always something there to remind me.

In the evening, I tell Mum about Ron's latest letter. She thinks he's pulled the pain barriers up.

'How's Grace, now?' Mum asks, changing the subject.

Guilt strikes like a knife every time someone mentions her name.

'She seems better. At least she's got Danny, that's something.'

She found Danny on a chat-line phone-in. They seem to have a lot in common and I'm happy she's found a diversion. But I don't think the guilt will ever leave me where Grace is concerned.

TUESDAY 4 AUGUST 1987

I phone Ron late afternoon. He sounds happy to hear my voice and we make arrangements to meet at Trafalgar Square tomorrow at eleven. He's managed to sell his camera for £150 so he has enough money to last him until he goes back on the eighteenth. To my disappointment, he still wants to go sooner, but they've told him there are no flights available.

Thank God.

He's been out for a drink with some of his mates so he wants to get his head down. He also says he has the use of a van and might go down the West Country next week for a few days to clear his head – even his family are beginning to get him down now.

Mal's working away and Carol's out so I collect Grace and bring her back for dinner with me. She looks around and casts a critical eye over the décor. She doesn't talk much except to say Claire is staying the night with her. I ignore the twinges of guilt for not being there. Grace seems OK though, in fact they're looking forward to having the house to themselves.

I try to discuss what she'll do when she finally leaves school. I would like her to do a design course at college, I've always harboured a wish that she follow in my dad's footsteps. She's always had an artistic flair and I would hate to see her waste her talent. But she's non-committal; her head is full of Danny.

I take her home and come back, have a bath and prepare myself for tomorrow. I want to look my best – it may be the last time I see Ron.

How will I feel? How will we be together? Will he look any different?

I hear Carol return but I'm not in the mood to go downstairs and chat. I play *Your Wildest Dreams* in my room and relive that first day.

He loses his woman again. That's not going to happen to us.

WEDNESDAY 5 AUGUST 1987

I wake up to a sunny morning – a good omen. I eat my breakfast in the kitchen, the timer on the heating/hot water boiler comfortably ticking away. Then I run upstairs to make the last minute adjustments to my appearance. Not wanting anything to distract my attention from Ron, I choose comfortable clothes. New jeans that hug my body like a glove, white tee shirt and white loafers. One last glance in the hall mirror. A deep breath.

This is it, then.

Feeling my guiding spirits hovering above me, I board the train. Everyone I see on the journey seems to have an air of expectation as if they sense my excitement.

Trafalgar Square. That first day back in April and all the weeks that followed flash before me like a fast film. Exposed in the open air, a soft wind blows and makes my skin tingle. Seven weeks have passed since I last saw Ron, and my heart soars as I watch him walking towards me. His smile warms my soul. I kiss him and will the day to stretch into infinity.

We go to Earls Court to pick up his ticket. He can't change it; it's still the 18th August. Sitting upstairs on the red double-decker, I show him my photos. He stops at the one with the sun glinting through the trees and stares at it.

'That's beautiful. You should enter it in a competition. Have it enlarged.'

I bask in his praise.

As we walk briskly we talk about how things have worked out. He admits that if he'd been able to get a job he wouldn't have wanted to go back. The second week I went to live with him he was very confused; it clouded his judgement. I get the feeling he wanted so much to impress me but he just couldn't live up to all he'd promised me, promised himself.

'I need to go to the Monument to get my AmEx tied up,' he says, as we walk. He jokes, 'You'll remember me for the bloke who made you walk everywhere!'

I'm desperately trying to stay upbeat but he makes it sound so final. How will I be able to live without Ron in my life? I know I only have him for a few more hours but I have to make the most of it. We talk all the time and both come to the same conclusion – it hasn't worked out this time, but who knows what the future holds?

I can tell by the way he looks at me and the way he holds my hand that he still cares. We walk across Westminster Bridge to a restaurant bar on the embankment, order a pot of Earl Grey and sit outside in the sunshine. He says he's going down to Dorset for a couple of days to clear his head; he's still a bit fuddled.

'I just want to be on my own without my family around, or you. Everything happened too quickly and we did everything arse-about-face. If I'd been in this country when you sent that fortieth birthday card, it would all have been very different, I'm sure.'

I swallow hard and close my eyes. The sun is like a balm to my sadness. We talk about what we've been up to recently.

'I hurt myself while I was playing cricket with Sally's boys. My own fault, I should've been more careful.'

I put my hand on his chest.

He looks at me in surprise, 'How did you know it was *there*?'

I smile. There are no words to express how I feel at this moment. It's a spiritual thing. He puts his hand on mine and looks at me intently. How I have yearned for that touch, that look! A wave of emotion rises up through my chest and settles at the back of my eyes, but I will myself to stay positive – I don't want anything to cloud this special day. I desperately want another chance but I know he's dead set on going back. Nothing I say will change his mind.

Waterloo station. The day has flown. I buy us both a gin and tonic and we sit in the stuffy crowded bar waiting for his train. I want to hold back the minutes. He's fidgety; gulps his drink. I know he's trying to soften the blow when he hastily says, 'Remember, friendship means everything. It hasn't worked out this time but who knows what the future holds? I'm coming back for Mum and Dad's golden wedding anniversary in two years' time, anyhow.'

I want so much to stay in the moment but my thoughts are straining at the leash wanting to rush headlong into the future.

'I'll probably be back for six months and want to come back here! Half of me wants to go and half of me wants to stay.'

Oh, I wish.

A case of the grass is always greener... I don't know if he really believes this or whether he says it to relieve the tension. I sit with my hand on his knee but he makes no attempt to hold it. I'm wishing for extra minutes, dreading that train coming in.

'I'll try and see you once more before I go back; if not, we'll talk.' He swallows another mouthful of drink and stares into his glass.

My heart is pounding, the time of departure drawing ever closer. He looks at his watch and downs the rest of his gin and tonic.

No! Not yet.

I search for something to say to stop him leaving, but my mind is dark and empty. He gets up, intent on getting his train, and I walk with him to the ticket barrier. He stops and turns to me. 'Remember,' he repeats, 'friendship means everything. We've got a lot of good memories.'

A slight hesitation then he kisses me with such feeling I know I will never forget this moment. My throat aches and I swallow down the impulse to cry. I know he won't want to remember me in tears. As he goes through the barrier he looks back once more, as if he's trying to imprint my image onto his memory.

Then he's gone.

EPILOGUE

I never saw Ron again.

I remarried on my fortieth birthday, put the episode with Ron to the back of my mind and started a new life. I knew in my heart that Ron and I would never be a couple, even if we met up again in the future.

He had a hard time settling back in Australia, living out of a suitcase. He wrote to me a few times while I still lived at Carol's, but as he didn't have a fixed address, I couldn't reply. But I spoke to him on the phone on a number of occasions when he was visiting family. I would get a very strong feeling that he was back in England and this would prompt me to phone Lottie. He always sounded excited to hear from me, and on hearing his voice I was always buoyed up for at least a week afterwards.

On New Years' Eve 2007, twenty years after our last goodbye, Sally texted me to say he was gravely ill in Sydney. He had cirrhosis of the liver. He ended his days in palliative care and I couldn't imagine him lying in bed racked with pain; he was always so full of life. Sally told me he didn't want anyone to see him – he wanted everyone to have the best of memories.

Ron died in February 2008 aged 61.

He remains locked in a special corner of my heart.

PLAYLIST

The Sheik of Araby.	Chris Barber.
Reach Out.	The Four Tops.
Gotta Get You Into My Life.	The Beatles.
Bolero	Maurice Ravel
The Big Country.	Jerome Moross
The Magnificent Seven.	Elmer Bernstein
Genghis Khan (1966 Film)	Dusan Radic.
Freight Train	Elizabeth Cotten
Stop in the Name of Love.	The Supremes.
Think of Me from The Phantom of the Opera.	Lloyd Webber
Rock Around the Clock.	Bill Hailey.
I Wanna Hold Your Hand.	The Beatles.
Your Wildest Dreams.	The Moody Blues.
The Streets of London.	Ralph McTell.
The Trap.	Ron Goodwin.
Errol's Bounce.	Errol Garner
The Other Side of Life.	The Moody Blues.
No One Comes Close	John Farnham

If you have enjoyed this book please write a review on

Amazon.co.uk

Thank you.

You can reach me at J.A.Newman@pobroadband.co.uk

Printed in Great Britain
by Amazon

18149039R00149